I0080156

THE YOUTH MENTORING PLAYBOOK

The Youth Mentoring Playbook

Copyright © 2024 Zachary Garza & John Barnard

All rights reserved. No part of this publication may be reproduced in a retrieval system, or transmitted in any form or by any means—electronic, mechanical, photocopying, recording, or otherwise—without the prior written permission of the publisher.

Scriptures taken from the Holy Bible, New International Version®, NIV®. Copyright © 1973, 1978, 1984, 2011 by Biblica, Inc.™ Used by permission of Zondervan. All rights reserved worldwide. www.zondervan.com The "NIV" and "New International Version" are trademarks registered in the United States Patent and Trademark Office by Biblica, Inc.™| Scripture quotations marked (NLT) are taken from the Holy Bible, New Living Translation, copyright ©1996, 2004, 2015 by Tyndale House Foundation. Used by permission of Tyndale House Publishers, Carol Stream, Illinois 60188. All rights reserved.

This manuscript has undergone viable editorial work and proofreading, yet human limitations may have resulted in minor grammatical or syntax-related errors remaining in the finished book. The understanding of the reader is requested in these cases. While precaution has been taken in the preparation of this book, the publisher and author assume no responsibility for errors or omissions, or for damages resulting from the use of the information contained herein.

This book is set in the typeface Athelas designed by Veronika Burian and Jose Scaglione.

Paperback ISBN: 978-1-955546-83-6

A Publication of Tall Pine Books
www.tallpinebooks.com

| 1 24 24 20 16 02 |

Published in the United States of America

THE YOUTH MENTORING PLAYBOOK

A 30-Day Guide *to* Invest
in the Next Generation

ZACHARY GARZA AND **JOHN BARNARD**
VOLUME ONE

"We live in a world where most people move at a place like they are swiping on a social media feed. What I love about John and *The Youth Mentoring Playbook* is that it encourages the reader to slow down, be present, and build intentional relationships that truly afford lasting discipleship opportunities. We need more content like this in our world!"

—MARK KOCH
Founding Global Director at *Ride Nature*
Fort Meyers, Florida

"Zach is uniquely able to fill a crucial need for Christian mentoring organizations. He offers encouragement for the work, easy-to-implement best practices, and he demonstrates the heart of Jesus for healing through relationships."

—AMY BEIGEL
Caregiver Experience Manager at *Prison Fellowship*
Charlotte, North Carolina

"*The Youth Mentoring Playbook* is a heartfelt exploration of the transformative power of mentorship, offering insight into how meaningful guidance can shape personal and professional growth. The stories shared are inspiring and relatable. Garza and Barnard offer practical strategies to understand and address the root causes of challenging behavior, advocating for empathy and patience. A must-read for anyone seeking to better understand the impact of positive influence on others' lives."

—LANNY WILLIAMS
Lifelong Coach/Mentor and Assistant
Director of Athletics at *Killeen ISD*

"The development of our children is vital to the future of our communities and cities. Love what Zach and John are doing here to strengthen our youth through mentoring and discipleship. I know this book will be a tool to help mentors make disciples through building relationships."

—DILLON MEEK
Former Mayor of Waco, Texas

"From the newest to the most seasoned mentor, connecting with your mentee can be a challenge. John and Zach have not only found a way to capture practical, applicable and effective ways for mentors and mentees to connect, but they have also created an approach to increase the mentor's impact. This book should be in every mentor's tool kit."

—DERRICK SIER
Founder of Reverb Mentoring and Director of
Leadership Development at Restore OKC
Oklahoma City, Oklahoma

"Three cheers for this practical guide for mentors! Zach and John share solid mentoring wisdom for Christians who want to serve others through mentoring, and the content is delivered in a winsome, bite-sized format making it relevant and easy to put into practice. Step up to mentor and use this playbook to strengthen every aspect of your game and your team."

—KAREN PEARSON
President at Kids Hope USA
Zeeland, Michigan

"Zach Garza lives his message. Mentoring isn't just an activity he does but being a mentor is who he is. The impact he has made and will continue to make is obvious and undeniable."

—AUSTIN MURRAY
College Pastor at Antioch Community Church
Waco, Texas

"John and Zach are two of the greatest leaders I know. I have been working with Youth for 13 years and yet these two still teach me so much! This book will equip you, challenge you, and encourage you to be the best mentor you can be."

—DEREK DAVIDSON
Resident & Family Pastor at *Harris Creek Baptist Church* Waco, Texas

"Having known Zach for almost 25 years and having watched him give his life and occupation to loving and mentoring young people, there is no one I would rather read on this topic than him. In this book you will hear from a man who has spent decades as a mentor, has experienced all the ups and downs of this calling, and has given his life to raising up others to do the same. For anyone in a mentoring relationship, this book should be in your library!"

—AUSTIN LAWRENCE
Lead Pastor at *The Well Church*
Abilene, Texas

"I love this book! It's short and to the point, but covers some powerful topics. One key lesson is that there is no such thing as a 'bad' kid—every child has goodness in them. Our role is to love them unconditionally, just as Jesus does. I was also deeply moved by the concept of the 'Hope Dealer,' which really resonates with many of the kids we work with today. As mentors, it's our responsibility to instill hope in young people, no matter the challenges they face. I'll be adding this book to our library—it's an excellent resource!"

—SACHER DAWSON
Executive Director at *Hope Farm*
Fort Worth, Texas

Dedicated to you the reader of this resource. You are the spotlight holder. The encourager who shows up & lives out their faith. The one who speaks into the life of a child without a paycheck, followers, likes, or fanfare, and yet continues to sow and reap, knowing the harvest is plentiful.

JOHN BARNARD

Dedicated to the Lake Highlands community and all who have made it possible for me to pursue the ministry of making disciples through mentoring. Without you, there is no way I would have had the opportunity to become a mentor, nor could I have made it my profession to encourage others to mentor kids in the name of Jesus.

ZACHARY GARZA

CONTENTS

INTRODUCTION

Who changed your life? What relationship got you to where you are today?

As much as we'd like to believe we are self-made, we did not get to where we are without a little help. Life is a team sport, not a solo competition. It's basketball, not golf.

Relationships change lives, and a mentoring relationship can be the perfect conduit for that change. As followers of Jesus, we want to use that mentoring relationship to teach our mentees skills to help them fulfill their potential. But more importantly, we want to teach them the ways of Jesus through intentional words and actions. After all, the Bible doesn't tell us to "go and make mentees," but to "go and make disciples" (see Matthew 28:19).

While sermons and teachings add value through the transfer of knowledge, only relationships produce lasting life change. The best gift Jesus gave his followers was *himself*. The same is true with us as mentors. But what does this look like, to give of ourselves? Jesus clued us in when He said, "The Son of Man came to serve, not to *be served*," (see

Matthew 20:28). We are to follow His lead. There is a phrase that we like to use, "Mentors shine the spotlight." Father Richard Rohr said the two types of leaders are those who stand in the spotlight and those who hold the spotlight on others. While the world needs both types of people, mentors are the latter. To shine the spotlight on our mentees means we get the chance to let them see who they really are; children of God destined for greatness through obedience to His plan for their lives.

Mentors, with a spotlight in hand, understand that it's not about them, but about those they are called to serve. It's about becoming the shoulders that others will stand on. The funny thing is, as we focus on others, we get better along the way.

This book was written for all mentors: organizational leaders, teachers, coaches, youth leaders, ministry staff members, and informal "everyday" mentors. The heart of this resource is a clear mentoring philosophy, backed by biblical principles, that helps you practically overcome common mentoring obstacles. This book is designed to serve you as you serve others over and over. Mentoring is not complicated, but that does not mean it's easy. We must be reminded of these principles often.

By providing insightful content with common language, our hope is that Christian mentoring organizations will find within these pages a resource to empower their volunteers and staff. Beyond that, it will help equip individual mentors with best practices and encouragement to know they are not alone in their mentoring struggles. We are committed to equipping and encouraging "investors-into-others" with practices that will guide them over the long haul.

The book is broken down into five sections within each topic. First we present the **problem**, which sheds light on common mentoring issues. Next we provide the **principle**, which is the foundation to overcoming the problem. This will be followed by the **passage**, laying down a biblical text to back our principle. For many topics, we add a **personal testimony** to reinforce the strategy—a story that you can talk about with others. Lastly, we give you the **practice**, providing workable, action steps to overcome the problem.

Are you short on material? Unsure of how to encourage your staff, volunteers, and the mentors in your care? Share these! You don't need the pressure of coming up with a pep talk or lesson all the time; it's right here for you. We learned many of these principles from other experienced mentors, and it's our joy to pass them on to you. Freely we've been given; freely we give.

Perhaps your mentoring organization can focus on one principle per week? Maybe they can be discussion starters to use with your staff and volunteers. You might even need content to pass along in a weekly newsletter. Great! The content here is available to share. Customize it in whatever way will be the most helpful for you and your unique environment. We want to encourage you to add texture to these principles and expand on them with your own mentoring stories and experiences. This book is not a stone monument to admire but clay in your hands to mold and shape to your unique circumstances.

We're all on the same team with the same goal; to love young people and help them know Jesus. The Lord can use you to transform a life, and this book will support you on your journey. We believe in you and know that the Lord loves to use people just like you to do amazing things for His glory. Your name can be the answer when someone asks your mentee, "Who changed your life?"

You can mentor.

IDENTITY-BASED VS. SKILL-BASED MENTORING

1

PROBLEM:

Mentors focus too much on what they can see and not enough on what they *can't* see.

What they can see: behavior, practical skills, grades, etc.

What they can't see: heart, hurts, how mentees see themselves, etc.

PRINCIPLE:

If a mentee's heart is not healthy, no amount of skills or knowledge will help them fulfill their potential.

PASSAGE:

"Above all else, guard your heart, for everything you do flows from it." (Proverbs 4:23)

PRACTICE:

- Build courage to overcome the awkwardness of speaking deep truths to the heart of your mentee

- Speak worth and value over your mentee by saying phrases like: "I love you just as you are, not as you should be," "I believe in you. You can accomplish anything you set your mind to", and "I really like being with you. Thanks for hanging out with me."

- Call out how you see the Lord working and moving in their life. For example, "You were really kind in that situation. That reminds me of Jesus. Great decision."

When most people think of mentoring, they think of teaching tangible skills to their mentee. Things like how to shake a hand, tie a tie, or create a job resume come to mind. The goal with this is to give them the skills needed to fulfill their potential, reducing mentoring to a *knowledge* issue. The idea is that providing more knowledge will fix the issue and help them flourish as a productive member of society. We call this skill-based mentoring, and there ain't nothing wrong with a little skill-based mentoring.

The issue is when we make skills the main thing, prioritizing handiness over identity. Let me explain. I'm not much of a handyman. I don't like using hammers and I have a hard time recognizing the difference between a screw and a nail. The worst part about my handyman insecurity is that my wife happens to be extremely handy. When something breaks, she fixes it. She has a pink hammer and a wide assortment of hardware.

As a man, this makes me a little insecure. I worry if anyone finds out, my man card may be in jeopardy.

One year, I made a vow to learn to be handier. And I did that by spending a ridiculous amount of money on some brand new, top-of-the-line tools.

My first job was to create another bookshelf for our living room. This one was going to be the bookshelf of all bookshelves. I went to Home Depot to get all the supplies and as I was putting the piece of wood in my minivan, I thought it felt rather heavy. It had to weigh about 50 pounds. Nevertheless, I took it home, sanded it, stained it, installed brackets on it, and found the perfect spot on my wall to hang it.

I felt so manly.

I grabbed some screws, got my drill, and hung this massive piece of wood. It looked pretty good and I was really proud of myself. I called my wife to admire it with me. I took a picture and sent it to my dad, loaded it up with books and called it a day.

A few weeks later, my wife and I were startled awake at 1 am by an incredibly loud noise coming from our living room. Terrified, I slowly walked toward the sound, baseball bat in hand, about to go Barry Bonds on this intruder. As I walked into our living room, I saw complete chaos. Books were everywhere and a twelve-foot piece of Cedarwood was laying on my coffee table. Massive holes were in the wall, ripped open by the brackets. My bookshelf had fallen. My first handyman project was a failure.

I guess I wasn't as handy as I thought.

I was spending time with the Lord a few days later and thinking about mentoring. I asked the question, "Lord, how can I equip our mentors with the best tools to love the kids we serve?"

He reminded me of the bookshelf and I pictured the complete mess. I retraced my actions and thought about how the accident occurred when this question popped into my head, "Zach, was the issue with your brand new DeWalt drill?"

"No way," I thought. "That thing is top of the line. There was nothing wrong with the tool."

"Then what was the issue?"

"Oh, man," I realized, "the issue wasn't with the tool at all. The issue was with the one using the tool. I simply didn't know what I was doing."

The Lord was asking me if as a mentor, am I creating a handyman or am I simply providing tools? That's a tough question to answer.

You see, just like my brand new drill, tools are no good if your mentee believes they are dumb or if they lack confidence and self-value. Knowing how to use a tool will not offset the pain of someone telling your mentee they won't amount to anything in life.

While providing tools and skills is a great thing, a better focus is on their identity—namely, how they see themselves and how God sees them. We must dispel the lies and replace them with truth. In this, we ensure that the foundation of our mentee is secure.

Although practical skills are very important, we must overcome the awkwardness and speak truth to the heart of our mentee. If they are insecure or believe false identities, we must speak identity to those lies. Be quick to use phrases like, "I love you just as you are, not as you should be", "I believe in you. You can accomplish anything you set your mind to", and "I really like being with you. Thanks for hanging out with me." Mentees need to hear you speak worth and value into them. It is nourishment for their soul and ointment on their wounds.

We want our mentee to see themselves how the Lord sees them, and we must remind them of that often. Call out how you see the Lord working and moving in their life. For example, "You were really kind in that situation. That reminds me of Jesus."

We have an opportunity to turn their negativity into a healthy perspective. We see the bigger picture, and we get to share that as we walk alongside our mentee. Mentors are gem cutters, taking the rough and shaping them into beauty so our mentees can reflect the light of their Heavenly Father.

We get to help them see themselves how God does—full of unconditional worth and value as a beloved child of God.

Oftentimes, mentors come to me and say, "My mentee doesn't want to learn what I'm trying to teach them." I respond, "That's because they don't believe they can do it... and no one likes to start something if they believe they will ultimately fail."

When they *believe* they can have success and grow, they will have intrinsic motivation to learn the skills. They will be hungry to become all that they can be because they believe in themselves and have someone believing in them. Only a person who believes they can improve will put in the work to actually improve.

So focus on the identity. Make sure they are seeing themselves rightly. Pump them full of hope and confidence by encouraging them relentlessly. Tell them how God sees them over and over again.

Then, *pow*, introduce the skills. Identity first, skills second.

NO SUCH THING AS A BAD KID

2

PROBLEM:

Once a mentee has repeated multiple offenses towards a mentor, it is human nature to give up on them as you label them an unfixable "bad kid".

PRINCIPLE:

Being a mentor requires us to emulate Jesus, meaning we love with an unconditional love.

PASSAGE:

"We love because he first loved us." (1 John 4:19)

PRACTICE:

- Remember our mentees have hurts in their past that cause unhealthy actions. They may act out because they lack attention at home or are angry because they experienced injustice as a child.

- Emulate Jesus, who loves us despite our repeated failures and sinful actions. It is our call to do the same with others.

- Focus on what they are doing right instead of what they are doing wrong. Encourage your mentee often. These kids often have more than enough people in their lives telling them about what they are doing wrong. May our words, actions, and non-verbal facial expressions say the opposite. We are not here to "fix a kid", but instead to love a kid.

They say "Don't judge a book by its cover." But I'm here to tell you, I judge every single book I've ever read by its cover. If a book has a bad cover, it's gonna be really hard for me to pick it up and give it a chance.

Unfortunately, judgment doesn't just apply to books. It can apply to our mentees as well.

As a former teacher, this would happen to me all the time. A new kid would walk in the door with his shirt tucked in and a high-and-tight haircut and I'd let them sit wherever they want without giving them a second thought.

A new kid would walk in the door with dyed hair, a shirt with a skull on it, and torn up jeans and I'd put them on the front row so I could keep an eye on them—watching them like a hawk.

It is really difficult to *not* judge a kid based on how they look.

If a kid has tattoos.

If they have a scowl on their face.

If they are dressed a certain way or have a certain kind of haircut.

If these things are true, the lies start flooding into my mind.

"This kid is going to be a problem."

"They're not going to listen to a thing I say."

"This probably isn't going to work. They are too far gone."

I know this is terrible to admit, but I have for sure judged a book by its cover. I still have to fight the initial negative thoughts when I have a bad first impression with a kid.

I am guilty of labeling some kids "a bad kid" before even speaking with them. But if there is one thing I have learned in my mentoring experiences, it is that there is no such thing as a bad kid.

There is, however, such a thing as a hurt kid.

The kid with a tattoo? Maybe it's a reminder of a loved one that they lost. Maybe it's a cry for attention.

The scowl on their face? Perhaps they've got a lot to be angry about. Maybe their dad left them. Perhaps they were the victims of racism or injustice; could be poverty, a teacher who didn't give them a chance, or the fact that life has not been easy for them compared to their peers.

Before you judge a kid, take the time to get to know them. Look past the haircut and the clothes and look at their heart.

Get curious. Learn their story. Ask good questions. Abandon assumptions.

If they are making bad decisions, like having sex, doing drugs, or using disrespectful language, their actions are saying something. They may be crying for help. Our mentees are searching.

One thing that helps me is to ask the Lord, "How do you see this child?"

And let us never forget we are dealing with a child.

When the Lord looks at your mentee, He doesn't see the actions. He doesn't see the bad behavior. He sees a son or a daughter—a precious child and a member of His family.

His heart abounds with grace, kindness, and acceptance, not of the actions, but of the person.

Christ doesn't see a bad kid. He sees a son or a daughter, full of value and worth. He sees a hurt kid and his heart goes out to them.

May we see the same as well. Let grace abound as we shed assumptions and take the time to truly get to know a child; a child who has possibly been through more than we can imagine.

RULE OF THREE

3

PROBLEM:

Some adults have abused their power and positions of authority. Because of this, all adults who spend time with kids must act in specific ways to elevate the safety of the child above all else.

PRINCIPLE:

Mentors stay above reproach in all environments to pursue relationships in the safest, most respectable way.

PASSAGE:

"A cord of three strands is not quickly broken." (Ecclesiastes 4:12)

PRACTICE:

- Depend on the Lord to create a way to build trust and facilitate deep conversation despite the inability to be alone with the child. Without compromise, follow best practices when spending time with your mentee.

- Be above reproach. When in doubt, contact the parent of your mentee and/or your mentoring organization.

- When picking them up for a car ride, it's vital that you let someone—either a parent or your mentoring organization—know when the mentee gets in the car with you and when you get to your desired location.

- Keep the door open. If you find yourself in a room alone with your mentee, make sure to let other people around know you are in there and keep the door open.

- Three is the magic number. When spending time with your mentee, try your hardest to get someone else to go with you; whether it's a mentee's friend or sibling or your own child, spouse, or friend.

- Avoid overnights. We recommend never doing an overnight with your mentee. If you find yourself in a situation where an overnight is going to happen, contact parents and ensure that you are surrounded with other people at all times.

It seems like there is a story in the news every month about an adult behaving inappropriately with a child who trusted them; usually it is a teacher, youth pastor, or a mentor. These stories always give me a sick feeling in my stomach, but it is important that we learn from these experiences to give our mentees the best experience possible and to protect all parties from potential harm.

Safety is the name of the game when it comes to mentoring. You always want to have safety on your mind when hanging out with your mentee. The first priority is always to keep the child safe. Another aspect of safety is following rules and procedures so you stay above reproach and free of any possible accusation. Yes, we focus first on keeping the mentee safe, but this is also about protecting you and avoiding any "their word against yours" scenarios. Even the perception of wrongdoing is enough to take out an entire mentoring relationship or organization.

One of the best ways to keep everyone safe in the mentoring journey is with *the rule of three*. The rule of three means there are always three parties involved when you are hanging out with your mentee. This third person can be a crowded place, a friend of yours or the mentee, or a member of yours or the mentee's family.

In our organizations, the rule of three is something we stress to every mentor, no matter age or experience.

If you ever find yourself in a situation that doesn't seem safe, do whatever you can to get out of that situation immediately and communicate the situation with either the parent or the mentoring organization.

We understand that relational depth and capital are vital to an effective mentoring relationship, but we must pursue those things within the boundaries of a safe relationship. If you want to talk privately, perhaps have it at a local park. If you need to have a hard conversation, try going for a walk around the neighborhood.

Yes, following safety guidelines will add some challenges to your mentoring relationship, just like stopping at a red light, wearing a seat belt, and driving the speed limit slow you down a bit. But they are vital to keep everyone safe.

The rule of three is a non-negotiable in any mentoring relationship with a minor. When in doubt, over-communicate with a third party, especially a parent. We want to stay above reproach for all parties involved. The stakes are too high when it comes to the safety of your mentee.

PRESENCE IS BETTER THAN PRESENTS

4

PROBLEM:

Just like in our relationship with God, we can stress what we do *for* our mentees instead of simply being *with* them.

PRINCIPLE:

Although gifts and unique experiences are fun, uninterrupted time spent with our mentees is enough to encourage them, build relationships, and cultivate an environment for life change.

PASSAGE:

"Then the word of the Lord came to Samuel: 'I regret that I have made Saul king, because he has turned away from me and has not carried out my instructions.' Samuel replied: 'Does the Lord delight in burnt offerings and sacrifices as much as in obeying the Lord? To obey is better than sacrifice, and to heed is better than the fat of rams." (1 Samuel 15: 10-11, 22)

PRACTICE:

- You are enough. As much time as you spend telling your mentee they are enough, remember also that you have value, just as you are.

- Put your phone away. Uninterrupted time means completely uninterrupted. Do whatever it takes to remove distraction from your meeting time.

- Value the mundane. Go on a simple walk with your mentee. Take them along as you do your weekly grocery shopping. Have them over for tacos with your family on Tuesday. Those basic tasks offer so many opportunities for us to listen well and speak truth to our mentees as we show them what it looks like to live as people of margin.

I love mentoring. I am the product of a healthy church youth group from the 80's and 90's where investing adults loved me well and gave me the chance to realize my identity and purpose within a group of teenagers who were my community during those formative years. I also was blessed by a youth minister named Troy who encouraged me and equipped me to the point that after high school (and some considerable wrestling with the call) I became a youth minister and committed to mentoring teenagers.

While Troy and the small group leaders at my church were well-prepared and intentional about our scheduled times together, they did me a greater service by living accessible lives and including me in them. After Wednesday night youth group, several of us would load up in Troy's little red Toyota pickup and get rides home (teenagers riding in the back of a single cab truck probably clues you in to the fact that this was over 30 years ago!)

I have never laughed harder than on those rides home sitting squished on that bench seat. I can't remember many of the Bible studies ever given during those times, but I remember the laughs and real conversations enjoyed on the fly while in Troy's truck. I had similar experiences with other youth workers as well because Troy committed to nurturing an intentional mentoring environment instead of a high-production program from the youth building stage.

As much as I love supporting teenagers and watching them realize their identity, purpose, and community in Christ, there is an element of mentoring I don't love–and that is the entertainment factor!

We may feel the pressure to keep our mentees engaged by entertaining them. Games and creative ideas and outings can make good memories for you and your mentee. But, if your initial meetings with your mentee included creative and ornate activities, you may begin to believe your mentee needs a firework show every time you meet.

A church-planter friend once said that when it comes to attracting potential church members, "Whatever it takes to get them will be what it takes to keep them."

Let that sink in for a minute.

If we spend energy thinking about extrinsic things to do for our mentee, we may suffer in the future to maintain a relationship that lasts. Instead, we should remember that we are enough! Just like your mentee, you have value just as you are.

In 1 Samuel 15, Saul is commanded by God to wipe out his enemies. But instead of doing so, Saul spares Agag the king and holds back some of the best livestock to make offerings to God later. Samuel reflects God's anger by telling him that obedience is better than sacrifice and that because Saul has rejected God's word, God is rejecting Saul as king. Intense!

This passage reminds us that God is serious about obedience. We must remember that what we do *with* God (obedience) is so much more important than anything we can ever do *for* Him (sacrifice)!

Time spent *with* your mentee is gold. Uninterrupted time means completely uninterrupted and 100% focused on your mentee's words and whatever they are communicating. Put your phone away and make eye contact. Listen actively, maintaining self-awareness of your resting face. Let them speak to a smiling face that is reflecting how Jesus feels about them!

Also, have a high value for the mundane. Go on a simple walk with your mentee. Take them along as you do your weekly grocery shopping. Have them over for tacos with your family on Tuesday.

Your presence is better than presents. You showing up just as you are and spending quality time with your mentee will help them feel important and valued. You don't have to be armed with cool toys. Simply invite them into the mundane of your life and let the Lord work. Like riding home with Troy in the little red Toyota, life-on-life living offers so many opportunities for us to listen well and speak truth to our mentees.

FILLED UP TO POUR OUT

PROBLEM:

We can get so hyper-focused on addressing our mentees' issues that we neglect our own.

PRINCIPLE:

If we are to be any good for our mentees, we must first address our own daily spiritual, physical, and emotional needs. We have to be filled up to pour out.

PASSAGE:

"How can you say to your brother, 'Let me take the speck out of your eye,' when all the time there is a plank in your own eye? You hypocrite, first take the plank out of your own eye, and then you will see clearly to remove the speck from your brother's eye." (Matthew 7:4-5)

PRACTICE:

- Prioritize your spiritual, emotional, and physical health. Are you committed to a regular devo schedule for personal growth? Are you reading books that keep you inspired? When was the last time you attended an encouraging conference? Who is mentoring you?

- Identify the unique ways that God pours into your life so you can pour out to your mentee.

- Use your worship as a conduit and be sure to go to God on a regular basis to get filled up! Be a resident worshiper, not a tourist!

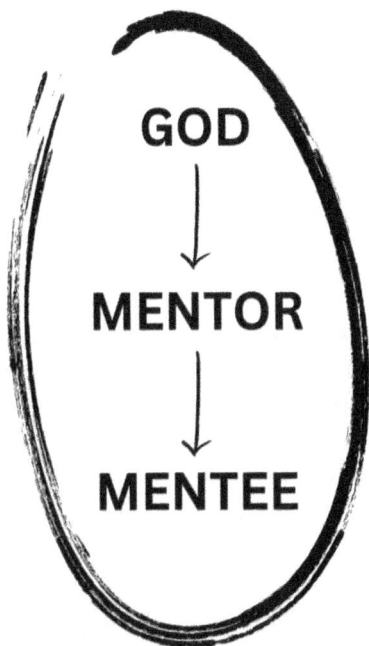

GOD
↓
MENTOR
↓
MENTEE

There is a favorite hiking trail in one of our state parks that was reopening after parts of it got washed out during a flood. The views along this trail are spectacular and the changes in altitude are enough to manage while still being a great workout for novice hikers. I invited my mentee, Josh, to join me and my family on the hike. Being deep into August, I was sure to tell Josh he needed to bring water for our long and hot day together as there were no stores or water sources out on the trail. I must have told him at least three times before that day he would need to bring a water bottle with him and each time he agreed he would.

Guess what? He didn't. But I saw that one coming, so I was sure to make a mental note to bring enough water for him and everyone else I was responsible for that day.

The bigger problem was I picked up the wrong pack that morning, so I didn't have any water for anybody! The old expression about one not being able to draw water from a dry well was real! Because of my lack of preparation, our trip was cut short.

By being ill-prepared for the day, I couldn't get myself or my mentee where I planned to go. Had we attempted the journey with no water, we would have suffered in many un-avoidable ways. Worry, doubt, and fear would have been stronger in my mind than being open to how God wanted to grow our relationship and enjoy a beautiful sunset.

That day was a tangible (and frustrating) reminder that if we are spiritually, emotionally, or physically dry, we won't be able to address our mentee's needs. Entering time with a mentee "full" means having the freedom and flexibility to address their issues without struggling with our own.

If you were to run the measuring stick down the well of your heart, where would you find the water line? Are you full or empty?

There are some important factors to consider when an-swering that question: Are you committed to a regular devo schedule for personal growth? If your mentee was as consistent in their quiet times, Bible studies, times of worship, and prayer life as you, would you say it's enough?

We must never ask our mentees to go somewhere we ar-en't willing to go ourselves.

Are you reading books that keep you inspired? Hopefully you're committed to a regular time in God's word over all other texts. However, there are incredible resources written by wonderful, Christ-centered authors that speak into many aspects of Christian growth and well-being. Ask your friends what they are reading. Sharpen your reading skills by committing to a book a month. Are you an auditory learner? Download audio books or listen to podcasts.

When was the last time you attended an encouraging conference? Christian conferences are great ways to learn from talented speakers and to worship with the Body of Christ at large. The energy levels at conferences hosted at churches and Christian organizations cannot be matched. Think of them as youth camp for adults!

Who is mentoring you? This can be a tough question for those of us who are committed to pouring into others without the luxury of having many who have poured into us. That being said, we never age out of needing a mentor! If you currently lack the presence of one who regularly pours into your life, begin by asking God to send someone your way who will equip and encourage you. You may find the Lord reveals someone who is already in your life that you had not previously considered. There are older and established Christ-followers just waiting to be asked to a weekly coffee meeting!

We must be filled up to pour out with our mentee, and this is a job that cannot be delegated. Be filled up with kindness, joy, and peace. Only then can we give those things to our mentee. Your relationship with the Lord, and everything you are doing to nurture that relationship, is preparing you to love your mentee with the love of Jesus.

PAUSE TO PROCEED

6

PROBLEM:

Uncertainty in our thoughts, motivations, and responses create hurtful or confusing situations with our mentees we may regret.

PRINCIPLE:

Our words should be so intentional and thoughtful that our mentees know they can count on us to say what we mean and mean what we say.

PASSAGE:

"My dear brothers and sisters, take note of this: Everyone should be quick to listen, slow to speak and slow to become angry." (James 1:19)

PRACTICE:

- Just wait. Give yourself time and space when making a decision. Don't let your mouth get out ahead of your brain. Once you feel you can make a decision that all your thoughts and emotions agree on, then say yes or no.

- Listen to Jesus. He said in Matthew 5 that we're foolish to make oaths on anything in heaven, on earth, or even on ourselves. Jesus instructs us to be practical. Simply say "yes" and "no" and then do what we say we're gonna do! That should be enough.

- Remember we are human. Sometimes we go back on our word. When those times happen, ask forgiveness from the person you've slighted. Try to make it up to them and finally, give yourself a break!

Treebeard, or Fangorn in Sindarin, is the tree-giant character in J.R.R. Tolkien's *The Lord of the Rings*. He is said by Gandalf to be "the oldest living thing that still walks beneath the Sun upon this Middle-earth." Treebeard lives in the ancient Forest of Fangorn; to which he has given his name. If you're a fan of the book or the movie, you'll remember that Treebeard takes forever to do everything. He walks, talks, and thinks slowly. When the Hobbits ask for his help in defeating Saruman, he and his fellow forest-dwellers take their time during council.

What mentors can learn most from Treebeard is how vital it is to seek clarity and certainty when making decisions. This can be a hard pill to swallow for many who mentor. Maybe you were raised in a lively household with highly opinionated family members who made quick decisions based on emotions. Perhaps your career or lifestyle leans toward chaos so it's hard to slow down and enjoy quiet moments of reflection.

There are times when we need to make quick decisions and take decisive action in a situation. However, we want to be careful not to put any unnecessary pressure on a situation, our mentees, or ourselves when considering how we mentor. The urgent things are not always the most important, and vice versa.

An example might be our mentee coming to us with a relational or spiritual issue. Maybe they are seeking an answer on whether they should break up with their boyfriend or quit a sport after struggling with a coach. The issue may be deeper still as they are asking about the reliability of scripture or integrity of church leadership.

Our mentees' questions and struggles are not clay pigeons they launch into the air expecting us to draw our six-shooters (Bibles) and instantly blow them out of the sky with a relevant verse!

It is okay to not have the answer in a moment's notice. It is okay to tell your mentee you are going to take some time and research the issue or prayerfully consider the answer. We teach our mentees a lot about how we value our words when we practice intentionality with them.

What's the best thing about being certain in what we do and say? The fact that we usually don't regret our decisions. Making a decision with all of who we are means we have considered the options and are comfortable moving forward. We're not second guessing ourselves and there's a wonderful freedom in that.

There will be limitless opportunities for you to practice consistency and to show integrity with your words and actions as you mentor someone. I hope you will make it a priority for your words to matter and that you will set a good example for this with your mentee.

Isaiah 55:11 reminds us that every word that goes forth from God's mouth does not return to Him void. God does not make empty promises! If He has given you a word on something, you can trust Him to make good on it. We can stand on God's word. After all, His word is His bond!

So, what would Treebeard do? First, make sure you are truly hearing your mentee when they share an issue or ask a question. Practice active listening. Ask questions to become better informed of the issue. Repeat the question back to them and have them validate your rewording. Next, if necessary, take time to think. Sit quietly. This shows your mentee you care about the issue (which means you care about them). When you are ready, give an answer. If you need more time to consider the matter, ask for that of your mentee.

Always, always, always follow up on the issue! Make a note in your phone. Your practicing sound and consistent decision making will speak volumes of how your mentee can value and practice it as well. Let's stand on that and reflect it by practicing consistency between what we do and say. The gap between what we do and what we say is called disillusionment for our mentees. Eliminating that gap is called building trust. Take your time, close that gap, and commit to stedfast, consistent speech and decision making.

WHO ARE YOU?

7

PROBLEM:

Our society places value on what someone does instead of who they are as a person. This approach to identity creates a child who thinks they have to perform to become valuable.

PRINCIPLE:

We have value and worth given by God through His grace; this is not earned by what we can do. Our identity as children of God is eternal.

PASSAGE:

"The Spirit himself testifies with our spirit that we are God's children." (Romans 8:16)

PRACTICE:

- Find a time to ask your mentee, "Who are you?" to teach them it is not *what they do* that counts, but *who they are*. The inside is more valuable than the outside.

- Remind your mentee often that they are loved no matter what and that they have a value and a worth as a child of God that can never be taken away due to performance.

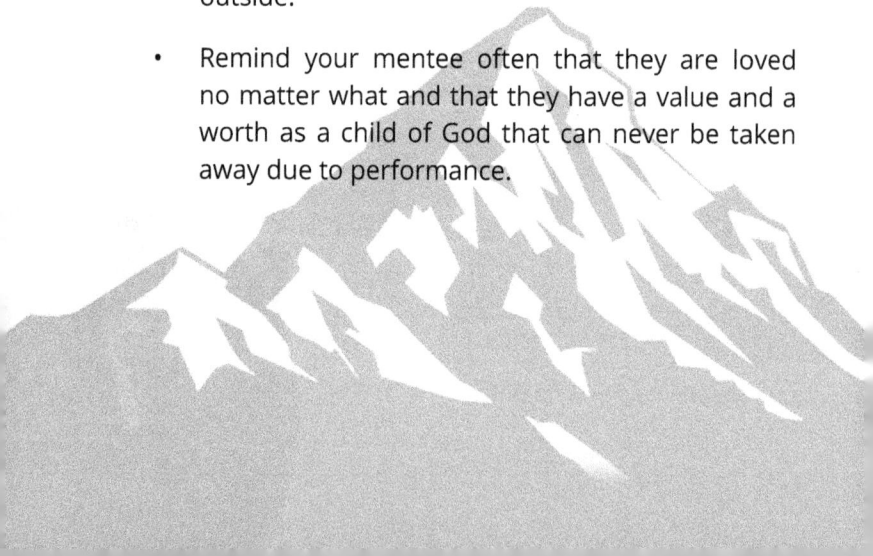

In 1990, H.G. Bissinger released the non-fiction book, *Friday Night Lights: A Town, a Team, and a Dream.* It tells the story of the 1988 Permian High School Panthers football team from Odessa, Texas, as they made a run at the Texas state championship. The book was adapted into a popular movie and two television series'.

A key player on the team was James Earl "Boobie" Miles. He was one of the best running backs in Texas; recruited by the top college programs in the country. During a preseason scrimmage, however, Miles incurred a serious knee injury that all but ended his football career.

There is a powerful quote from the book when Miles remarks to someone after his injury, "What am I gonna do if I can't play football? I ain't good at nothin'!" The issue larger than his injury was that he confused his identity with his purpose. While his community valued him for what he could do on the field, he struggled to find any worth in himself (a healthy identity) outside his performance as a running back (sole purpose).

In Miles' case, the downward spiral of life lasted many years after he unsuccessfully attempted to regain his former glory as a football player. As an adult, Miles went on to father four children who he would not raise. He was arrested multiple times and in 2023 was sentenced to 13 years in prison.

James Earl Miles was more than just a talented football player. He was a young man with most of his life ahead of him. God blessed him with strength and speed. He and his community developed and leveraged his gifts in football to make him successful at his position. Unfortunately, his story is void of anyone willing and able to nurture James' identity beyond the sport.

Our mentees are so much more than the temporary titles they carry, whether they are "football player" "academic all-star" or "talented musician." These roles only last for a time as life goes on. Yet, our mentees often wrap up their entire identity in them. How many times are teenagers making life-altering decisions based on their inability to see past their current struggles? It is our job as mentors to remind them that there is more to who they are than what they do.

Find a time to ask your mentee the simple question, "Who are you?" Their first answer may be to tell you their first name. Follow up your initial question with, "Ok, who is Robert?" When they give you an answer that includes something that includes their purpose rather than their identity, follow that answer with, "Excellent, now tell me who Robert the musician really is."

Playfully challenge your mentee when they choose to iden-tify themselves by an activity they love. Ask them how they would answer who they are if they could no longer play that sport or that musical instrument.

This exchange may lead to some awkward or funny looks from your mentee, but it will set the stage for what the mentee should learn through the question. You are teach-ing them it is not what you do that counts, but it is who you are. The inside is more valuable than the outside.

Remind your mentee often that they are loved no matter what and that they have a value and a worth as a child of God that can never be taken away due to performance.

"Child of God" is a title that best describes those who know Jesus as their savior. We do well to remind our mentees that it's the only title (and identity) that can't be taken from us!

WHAT ARE YOU DOING?

8

PROBLEM:

When our mentees don't understand that God has a good plan and unique purpose for their lives, they will accept the purpose and plan society deems important.

PRINCIPLE:

As our mentees walk out their identity as a child of God, He reveals his unique purpose and gives them the courage to follow His plan for their lives. The more we know our mentees, the better we will be at speaking into their purpose.

PASSAGE:

"'For I know the plans I have for you,' declares the LORD, 'plans to prosper you and not to harm you, plans to give you hope and a future.'" (Jeremiah 29:11)

PRACTICE:

- Observe and identify your mentee's giftings and interests. Maybe have them take some personality tests to draw out their unique talents. Find others who share similar talents to give them a picture of what they can become.

- Find ways to develop and display that potential to guide them into their unique God-given purpose for their lives.

- Launch and encourage them. Know what stage you are in and act accordingly. Your role will change as the mentee matures.

Step	Role	Goal	Pending	Description
Step One	Scout	Observe	Identify	Watch and call out mentees' unique gifts.
Step Two	Coach	Develop	Display	Develop those gifts and find ways to spotlight them.
Step Three	Promoter	Launch	Encourage	Push them out of the nest and encourage them when times get tough.

I met Troy when I was in eighth grade. He had just been hired as the youth minister at the church I was beginning to attend. Like a lot of youth ministers back then, he was a good athlete, and I can remember playing a lot of basketball with him.

The best thing Troy did for me in those early days of youth group was to let me and my friends ride our skateboards at church on Wednesday nights. He knew that I loved skating and that if given the chance to ride there, I'd be at Wednesday nights every week to take part in Bible study. Once we really got to know each other, Troy started asking me to do skits for the church and lead from the stage during youth camp. He literally gave me a stage to perform on and that made me see the connection of who I was and how I could live my purpose for the Lord.

The peak of my skating ability was my senior year in high school. During that time, Troy organized a trip where a group of us went to Dallas and put on a demo that included skating with locals and a gospel presentation. That trip was the first time I drew a direct line between skating and ministry.

Some years later, Troy would be instrumental in helping me to start a skateboarding ministry while I was in college. He also increased my responsibilities, and I learned what it meant to serve and lead in the church. Even today, Troy continues to be an encouragement in my mentoring ministry, making sure we have funds needed to print Bibles that we give away at skateboarding camps.

OBSERVE AND IDENTIFY!

While Troy is talented and one of a kind, the best things he ever did for me were simple; he spent enough time with me to know who I was and then made sure I had opportunities to find my purpose.

All mentors can do that for their mentees as they spend time with them and learn what makes them tick. Once you know what your mentees love, find ways to show them they can use their interests and giftings to worship God through them. Spend time observing and identifying your mentee's giftings and interests. When talking about purpose, you may consider having them take a personality test that emphasizes their unique talents. Find others who share similar talents to give them a picture of what they can become.

DEVELOP AND DISPLAY!

Find ways to develop and display your mentee's potential to guide them into their unique God-given purpose for their lives. This is a great time to introduce your mentee to a professional or expert in a field they have expressed interest in. Go on a field trip! Make memories together as your mentee is exposed to a new world. Troy leveraged the youth group stage and created a mission trip for me to learn this lesson. What resources are at your disposal?

LAUNCH AND ENCOURAGE!

This is an area where mentors can learn from parents. While children grow and become more autonomous, parents must adjust from the role of overseer to support. Mentors can experience some of the same needed adjustments when their mentees move on to college or get married. The mentor is still needed, but the role shifts to meet the need. Launching our mentee means we allow them to grow in some areas outside our direct supervision and control. Yes, this time can be scary! Yet we trust the Lord's sovereignty and our mentee's judgment. May we all find ourselves as seasoned mentors launching our mentees into a new chapter of their lives! That is when purpose becomes realized and identity becomes solidified.

INVITE AND INTRODUCE

9

PROBLEM:

We live in a time where it is harder than ever to connect with people, and that is especially true with your mentee.

PRINCIPLE:

As people, we were made to live life with each other. Community should flourish in all areas of life. We must be intentional and persevering to make that happen.

PASSAGE:

"Therefore encourage one another and build one another up, just as you are doing." (1 Thessalonians 5:11)

Practice:

- Assess and leverage your network and resources to create opportunities to help them develop and launch. Use your relationships to help your mentees experience the power of community to help you become all that you were made to be.

- Introduce your mentee to positive adults who are similar to them. Give them someone they can look at and say, "I can be that!"

- Ask, "Who do I need to introduce my mentee to?" or "What experiences can I create to help them fulfill their purpose?"

- Inviting your mentee into your community, while simultaneously leveraging your community to help your mentee fulfill their God-given purpose. When you hang out with your friends, invite them! This could give them a group of people to champion them.

Have Healthy Relationships & Network →	Invite your Mentee into your world and introduce them to your people →	Mentees Experience the Power of Community →	Creates Opportunities, Relationships, and Open Doors →	Creating the Best Chance of Fulfilling of Mentee's Purpose

You ever heard the saying, "It's not what you know, but who you know"? The older I get and the more I reflect upon my life, the more that saying proves to be true. But as a young man, I had absolutely no idea of the power of community.

Simply put, life is a people game. There is no one out there who is 100% self-made. We all needed a little help to get where we are going. In my journey to becoming a mature adult, I had several key figures along the way.

I had a college professor named Bob who was the first man in my life that I remember taking an interest in me. He made me feel loved by his consistent presence. He gave me a job, always made time to talk, and invited me into his home. He also introduced me to Dan, who gave me my first job out of college.

Bob encouraged Dan to interview me to work as a year-long youth intern at his church. It was during this year that the Lord humbled me and allowed me to hit rock bottom in the kindest way possible. It was also at this church that I met my friends Joel and Randy.

Joel and Randy were about the same age as me, but they were light years ahead of me spiritually and in maturity. Randy put his finger in my chest and challenged me to stop acting like a knucklehead, while Joel gave me an inside perspective on being a godly, young husband and leader. Joel was also one of my first Christian peers that I wanted to be like.

After the church internship was over, I needed to find a job. That's when my college roommate Mark called me and told me he had a teaching and coaching position for me. That's how I got my first real job as an educator.

It was during my teaching journey that the Lord captured my heart and set it on fire for building relationships with kids from hard places. I got serious about my faith and found a mentor, a man named Steve who taught me how to love the Lord with all my heart. I also met a community leader named Greg, who encouraged me to start a mentoring organization. He became my first board member and his belief in me put me on the path that I'm on today.

And the list goes on and on.

Bob. Dan. Joel. Randy. Mark. Steve. Greg...those are just a few men who shaped and influenced me. Without them, who knows where I'd be?

The point is: God used my community to transform my life. And He can use you and your community to transform your mentee's life.

While I value education and hard work, almost every opportunity I have had in my life has been because of who I knew, and who they knew.

When I needed a job after college, Bob vouched for me. He called Dan and told him "Give this kid a shot." Bob extended his network to me, and it gave me an opportunity I may otherwise never have had. Greg not only made time to help me launch a mentoring organization, but he invited his network to join our board and to give at our first fundraiser. His relationships became my relationships, and for that I am forever grateful.

Imagine if I didn't accidentally fall into relationship with Bob? What if I just stayed in my room all day and played video games instead of getting out there and meeting people? I'd probably still be living with my mom, but instead the community I found helped launch me into adulthood. Isolation is deadly. It is not good for man to be alone.

Today, it is harder than ever to build relationships. Technology, busyness, and societal differences are just a few obstacles that sit in the road of relationship. Your relationship with your mentee may be one of the few adult relationships that they have. Know that, and use it to help them become all that God created them to be.

Model healthy relationships to your mentee, inviting them to be around other positive adults and introducing them to people who can help them flourish. Be intentional about seeking out experiences or relationships that could be beneficial to their growth and maturity.

One day, when someone asks your mentee, "How did you become who you are today? How did you get here and who helped you become successful?" a little smile will creep up on the corner of their mouth as they mention your name and they describe all the people and opportunities you introduced them to.

It's not about what you know, but who you know. And your mentee is blessed to know someone like you.

FIND YOUR TRIBE

10

PROBLEM:

Mentors often find themselves mentoring in isolation, which is a prime opportunity for the enemy to attack you with lies and discouragement.

PRINCIPLE:

We need to be surrounded by other believers who can encourage us when times get tough and to remind us of the "why" behind our decision to mentor.

PASSAGE:

"And let us consider how to stir up one another to love and good works, not neglecting to meet together, as is the habit of some, but encouraging one another, and all the more as you see the Day drawing near." (Hebrews 10:24-25)

PRACTICE:

- Find fellow mentors! Meet with them often. These people are in the game with you, they will understand your challenges and be able to provide comfort and wisdom when you need support.

- Invite your community into your mentoring journey. Tell your friends and family that you are mentoring. Give them permission to hold you accountable along the way.

- Submit to a mentoring organization and make time to invest into their trainings. The job of a mentoring organization is to support you on this journey. If there is a mentoring organization or movement in your community, consider joining their efforts.

If you've ever hiked up a mountain, you know it is no easy endeavor. Sure, there are easy parts but plenty that are just plain challenging. Storms can pop up, obstacles can block a path, and footing may not always be certain. The times of fun are often sandwiched between times of difficulty. But if you stick it out, the view is always worth the struggle it took to get there.

One thing I know to be true about climbing a mountain is it is always easier when you do it with other people.

People can pick you up when you fall down, encourage you when you get tired, and celebrate with you when you hit a checkpoint. People can champion you to do what you set out to do.

The same is true with mentoring; it's always better when you do it with others.

Mentoring alone is difficult. Why? Because oftentimes the "wins" in mentoring are few and far between. I have found that most mentors experience discouragement at some point in their journey. And when discouragement hits, it's usually downhill from there, especially when you are mentoring alone with no one to encourage you or pick you up when you fall.

But mentoring is all about persevering. It's all about continuing to show up over and over and over. It's about, like Jesus with us, overcoming the hard and being there for your mentee no matter what.

As a former mentoring executive, I would see mentors laboring in isolation all the time. I'd invite them to a training but they would be too busy. We'd call them on the phone to check in and it would always go to voicemail. They wouldn't show up to events because they'd miss the big game.

I knew it was only a matter of time before they'd quit because they didn't invest into a mentoring tribe. Whether you are starting your mentoring relationship or are a mentoring veteran, it's always a good idea to surround yourself with people who can help you.

The best mentors have a tribe. These are people who encourage them, ask them about their mentee, and who they can vent to when they experience hardships.

Here are some potential key members of your mentoring tribe and how they can assist.

AN ORGANIZATION (CHURCH / NON-PROFIT / SCHOOL)

- Provide you with best practices
- Create events to participate in
- Hold you accountable

FAMILY

- Cheer you on and celebrate when good things happen with your mentee.
- Help share the load, as they build relationships with your mentee.
- Pray for your mentee.

FRIENDS

- Mentoring in a small group is an excellent way to

team up to advance the Kingdom. You already live life together. Might as well do it on a mission.

- Like having an assistant coach. They might have expertise where you don't.

- They provide one more adult for the mentee to look up to.

YOUR TRIBE CAN:

- Help you stay encouraged.

- Speak truth when you are believing lies.

- Create a safe place to vent about hard times.

- Hold your proverbial mentoring arms up when they get tired like aaron did with moses.

- Give you new ideas on how to engage with your mentee or how to overcome an obstacle with your mentee.

- Help open up opportunities for your mentee.

- Pray for you and pray with you.

- Champion you to stay in the mentoring game for the long haul.

- Provide respite if you have a difficult season or unforeseen circumstance pop up.

Just like climbing a mountain, or going on any journey, it is better with a tribe of people. Mentoring for the long haul is easier when you are surrounded by people who love you and who are *for* you.

So find your tribe. Be open about your mentoring needs, opportunities, struggles, and victories. Share the load and allow others to hold your arms up when you get tired. There is an old saying that "a burden shared is a burden halved or doubled, depending on who you share it with." Build your tribe and find people who reduce the burden and increase the joy of your journey. Mentoring is *always* better with a team in your corner.

THERE'S NOTHING RANDOM ABOUT ACTS OF KINDNESS

11

PROBLEM:

Life gives us many opportunities to exercise genuine kindness, but how often are we striving to show it to, and in front of, our mentees so they value it?

PRINCIPLE:

Healthy mentors prioritize developing the spiritual fruit of kindness and are intentional about spotlighting kind words and actions to teach their mentees practical ways to be kind.

PASSAGE:

"But the Holy Spirit produces this kind of fruit in our lives: love, joy, peace, patience, kindness, goodness, faithfulness, gentleness, and self-control. There is no law against these things!" (Galatians 5:22-23 NLT)

PRACTICE:

- Put kindness on their radar. Intentionally share unique ways that you experienced the kindness of others (or ways you were kind this week) setting an example for your mentee to follow.

- Ask questions like, "Where did you experience kindness this week?" or "How were you intentionally kind this week?" This can be done each time you connect.

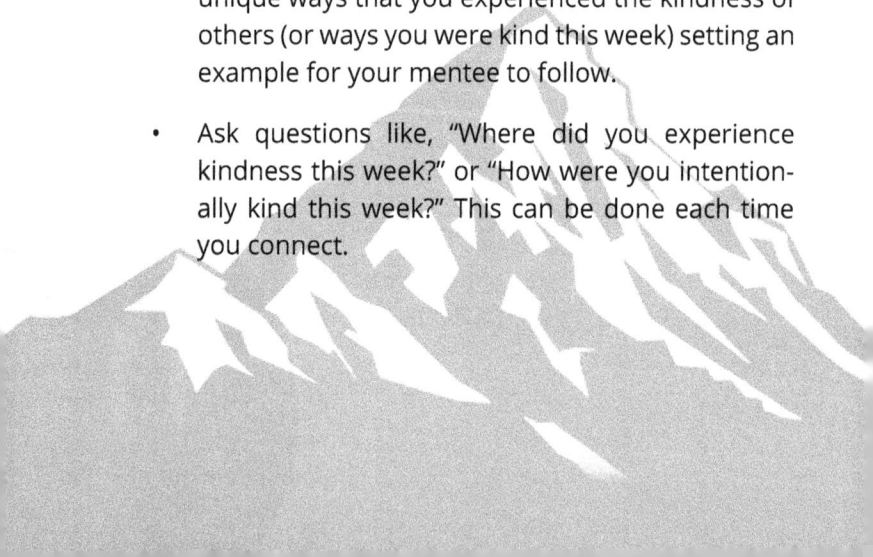

Kindness has that middle-child syndrome. Yes, it's a fruit of the Spirit but it's wedged there between patience and goodness and doesn't get the press that self-control enjoys. We have a funny relationship with the word. We know that we are supposed to be kind. We know a few people who we would describe as kind. But if we're being honest, how much do we really think about the character trait? Do we really STRIVE for kindness? I don't think we do. I think we're prone to relegate it to "random acts of kindness" or consider it to be the brand of a granola bar. (There is even a "Be Kind" coffee shop in my city.)

But how often are we intentionally looking to shape our character by seeking out ways to be kind? To take it a step further, how often are we talking to our mentees about kindness?

While mentoring, we gravitate towards focusing on the big things like grades, major sins, or future plans. But, what about kindness? Do we forget it because we believe it is a quality that some need and others don't? Does kindness make us quiet, meek, and timid? Do we take kindness for granted?

King David didn't. After David recounted all his many savage military triumphs in 2 Samuel 8, we find him sitting on his throne asking himself and everyone around him "is there anyone left in the house of Jonathan that he can show *kindness* to?" (see 1 Samuel 1:9).

Kindness was David's goal and he was intentional about spreading it to others. David prioritized kindness, realizing it was a commitment he made to Jonathan and he wanted to make good on his word.

The fruit of kindness is not timidity and weakness—it's absolute strength. It draws us to consider others better than ourselves and serve them well despite the circumstances. That takes strength and resolve. It takes courage and confidence. We should be striving for kindness to be ingrained in our hearts and on display for our mentees to see and take on as parts of their character. So, how can we be like David and prioritize kindness? Here are three simple steps to take:

1. *Think Kindness.* Most battles we fight are in the mind. Does Jesus have access to your thought life? Is He holding your thoughts captive? Are you meditating on God's word? Do you strive to have self-control in your thought life? We all get bugged by people who aren't like us. Next time you think a hurtful thought about someone you don't see eye-to-eye with, stop and center on one redeeming quality about the person no matter how long it takes. Ask the Lord to show you what He sees in that person. He or she is an image-bearer. God loves them. Jesus died to make things right between them and the Father.

2. *Speak Kindness.* Allow yourself to use kind words when speaking to and about people. Bite your tongue when you need to. Kindness is caught not taught! Your attitude when speaking to your mentee is contagious. The Bible says we are to be quick to hear, slow to speak, and slow to anger. When you feel yourself speaking overly critical about someone—stop! If your mentee hears you speak critically of a person, make sure you apologize for doing so and make it right!

3. *Do Kindness.* Act on the Spirit's prompting, especially when it's inconvenient! Practice kindness and see the benefits. I promise you'll want more of it in your life. Let your mentee see and hear about these occurrences, not out of pride or self-righteousness but as an example. Designate a time with your mentee where you share how you both showed intentional kindness to someone that week.

Make the kindness challenge something you and your mentee can do together. Challenge each other and encourage each other! It will be a fun and bonding experience. Remind your mentee that kindness does not have to be some major event like rescuing the neighborhood cat from a tree or pulling someone out of a burning building. It could be writing a thank you note, helping an elderly person carry groceries, writing a positive review, holding a door open, or complimenting a stranger.

KEEP THE MAIN THING THE MAIN THING

12

PROBLEM:

There is a temptation to make disciples of ourselves instead of making a disciple that looks like Christ.

PRINCIPLE:

God has uniquely made your mentee to worship, experience, and follow Him in specific ways and contexts that may or may not resemble our experiences or preferences.

PASSAGE:

"If anyone would come after me, let him deny himself, take up his cross, and follow me." (Mark 8:34)

PRACTICE:

- The main thing is following Jesus. Full stop. Toss preferences and your personal comforts out the window. It's His presence in our lives that gives us the motivation to deny ourselves, the power to take up our cross, and the willingness to follow!

- Reflect Jesus as a mentor and pray that your mentee follows you as you follow Christ.

- Celebrate the unique way your mentee follows Jesus. Your mentee is different from you and God is working in his or her life in different ways than He worked in your life. It is worth celebrating your mentee's uniqueness and how God wired and is using them. Don't get hung up on the small things.

Children love kinetic lessons. While mentoring in elementary schools, we would have kids trace out their silhouettes on a large piece of butcher paper. Students would fill in the spaces with what "a Christian looks like." It was hilarious to watch the paper person come to life wearing a Christian bookstore t-shirt, a WWJD bracelet, carrying multiple bibles and concordances in hand. They might be wearing their Sunday best while holding a John 3:16 sign.

This exercise gave the children a chance to think about how preconceived notions affect our definitions and preferences. Some of the biggest issues that plague our society can be traced back to prejudice and stereotyping.

We as mentors are wise when we refuse to take a one-size-fits-all approach to Christianity. We must remain flexible in our definition of what a follower of Christ looks like. We are trying to build disciples of all shapes and sizes. What does it for you may not do it for them.

Throughout recorded time, generations have struggled to appreciate and understand each other. It's not that we have differing goals of peace and prosperity, it's just that we vary in how we communicate and reach these goals. It's easy to get caught up in the words our mentees use and the clothes they wear—especially when we don't understand or appreciate the differences. Nevertheless, we must keep the main things the main things. Knowing the difference between the nonnegotiable and preference is key. Healthy and confident mentors don't get caught up in minor issues. They focus on emulating the actions of Christ: love, service, and obedience. Most importantly, we don't want to "put them in a box" in how they worship or experience the Lord.

Christ-followers come in all shapes and sizes. There is absolutely no way to know indefinitely how a person relates to Jesus by looking at and judging their outward appearance.

There are, however, three criteria we know a Christian must meet to fit the bill. They come from Jesus' words in Mark 8:34, "If anyone would come after me, let him deny himself, take up his cross, and follow me."

1. *Denying yourself.* What a powerful trait for the Christian! To deny yourself is to know your cravings, comforts, and anything that will keep you from God, and saying *no* to them. Self-denial is all about sacrifice! It is a daily choice we make to forgo our own motives and actions in favor of the Lord's. The Bible compares this contrast between us living by the cravings of our bellies versus living with a heart fully submitted to Jesus. To help your mentee understand this point, share about specific things you have denied yourself in the past. Use discernment during this time but also be honest. The goal is to show how self-denial strengthened your faith.

2. *Taking up our cross.* The Cross of Christ is also our calling in life, and I know that sounds heavy. We follow Jesus' example when we realize our *purpose* and live in obedience to what He has for us. Unlike Jesus, we don't take up a cross that offers salvation for others. We take up a cross out of obedience to God so we can do the work He has planned for us in a real and unique way. Be prepared to talk about specific crosses you have taken up in your faith journey. Some are seasonal and some transcend circumstances and years.

3. *Following Jesus.* This is the best part. Imagine God telling us to deny ourselves, get to work on this earth for Him, but then Him leaving us with no direction or guidance! That's crazy! We would be lost. Instead, Jesus says, "I have a plan and I will be revealing it to you daily as we walk through life together." Remind your mentee constantly that Jesus wants to spend time with them. Tell your mentee that nothing pleases the heart of God more than a close relationship as we abide in Him!

When your mentee realizes they have been given unique gifts and preferences, they will be free to worship in Spirit and truth (see John 4:24)! As we lean into the heart of God through our individuality, we grow in our ability to let others do the same. Many parts. One Body. One Spirit.

WORDS MATTER

13

PROBLEM:

Our words have the power to radically bless and transform a life, but they also have the ability to destroy and tear down. Flippant, unthoughtful, or impatient words can damage our mentee's emotions and well-being.

PRINCIPLE:

There is a permanence to our words that we need to be extra careful about when it comes to how we speak to and about our mentees.

PASSAGE:

"We all stumble in many ways. Anyone who is never at fault in what they say is perfect, able to keep their whole body in check. When we put bits into the mouths of horses to make them obey us, we can turn the whole animal. Or take ships as an example. Although they are so large and are driven by strong winds, they are steered by a very small rudder wherever the pilot wants to go. Likewise, the tongue is a small part of the body, but it makes great boasts. Consider what a great forest is set on fire by a small spark." (James 3:2-5)

PRACTICE:

- Choose your words wisely. Think before you speak. Your mentee is like a court reporter; they remember every word you say on the recorder in their brain. Know your audience, realize the context, and read the room! One practice is to ask yourself, "Would I say this if my mentee's mother was sitting next to me?"

- Realize that your intent is hard to measure. How many times have you had to say, "That isn't what I meant!" or "I was just joking." Our intent is a very weak defense. What our mentee *heard* is more important than what we *meant* to say.

- Get ready to say, "I'm sorry." Our mentees learn more about what it means to be a Christian during times of conflict and restoration than they do when times are easy, everyone is friendly, and circumstances are optimal. Be transparent. Model a peacemaker mentality and approach to relationships.

We've all done it. We have said something like, "Wow, Brian is the best. He is such a good kid." You may think there's not a thing wrong with that statement. But what about this one, "Geez. Brian is the worst. He is such a bad kid." While we wouldn't think to say that *about* or *to* a kid, we should at least recognize that both statements exist on the same spectrum of thought and action.

But what's the worst part of thinking about someone (or something) as being "bad"? Well, bad things don't go back to being good! Nothing in your refrigerator that goes bad gets good again, no matter how many Bible studies those cartons of milk attend! If we label a kid as bad or problematic, how often does that kid overcome that stigma?

There is a permanence to our thinking and words that we need to be extra careful of when it comes to how we speak about our mentees! We have focused a lot on how we speak to our mentee, but what about when we speak about them to other people? Kids often become the words that we speak over them.

Something I love about my wife, Mandi, is how she takes up for me. Not that she's out getting into barroom brawls over my reputation. But as we've probably all experienced, there are times in our nuclear and extended families that someone says a harsh or critical word about someone else. Mandi sees it as her responsibility as my wife to take up for me to ensure no one speaks poorly of me.

Sadly, that's not the case in all marriages. Some spouses are highly critical, dismissive, or even offensive when they talk about their significant other. I'm happy to say that I've enjoyed Mandi's conviction over this matter and discovered it's made me aware of any time someone (even one of our kids) speaks negatively about her.

So how do we consider this approach to being life-giving with our words when talking about our mentees?

We start by admitting that no kid came out of the womb with the doctor's saying, "This one is no good!" There are, unfortunately, some very unhealthy kids out there who had to endure trauma or abuse and who lacked the basic care and attention that many of us enjoyed during our formative years. People have been saying bad things about them for most of their lives. Let us be different. Let us focus on the good. Let us commit to loving our mentees well and shining the spotlight on what they are doing right. Our words matter and can give life. We may be the only people in our mentee's life saying good things about them.

Choosing our words wisely starts with thinking before we speak. Your mentee is like a court reporter; they remember every word you say on the hard drive in their brain. Know your audience, realize the context, and read the room! One excellent practice is to ask yourself, "Would I say this about my mentee if his mother was sitting next to me?"

We must also realize our intent is hard to measure. This might be an issue for you if you're constantly saying, "That wasn't what I meant!" or "I was just joking." Our intent carries very little weight in the real world. It doesn't matter what you meant to say, it only matters what your mentee heard!

Always be ready to say, "I'm sorry." Our mentees learn more about what it means to be a healthy Christian during times of conflict and restoration than they do when times are easy, everyone is friendly, and circumstances are optimal. Be transparent. Model a peacemaker mentality and approach to relationships. If you're feeling convicted about a harsh word you spoke to someone about your mentee, go back and apologize for what was said. You'll feel better and your listener will happily forgive you for the infraction.

Finally, we want to recognize that troubled and unhealthy youth can be a challenge to connect with, much less fight for! That's true even when you can agreeably nod your head to all these healthy reminders about what's at stake. When you feel yourself reacting harshly or letting a mean word rise to the surface, that is when you will want to find a place for those emotions and reactions outside of labeling or criticizing your mentee. This is when journaling can be very helpful. It gives you a chance to put feelings into words and before you know it, you'll find yourself laying your cares at the feet of Jesus.

ALWAYS A REASON WHY

14

PROBLEM:

Mentors get frustrated with their mentee's negative behavior and struggle to understand why their mentee is acting out.

PRINCIPLE:

We must stop, get curious, and take the time to learn our mentee's past to get perspective on how their unhealthy actions are possibly the result of their unmet needs.

PASSAGE:

"Get wisdom, get understanding." (Proverbs 4:5)

PRACTICE:

- *Get curious.* Curiosity creates opportunities to get to know your mentee better. Ask a ton of questions to try to figure out your mentee as best as possible. Your mentee may seem annoyed by your questions, but deep down they value your pursuit of knowing them better.

- What is my mentee really saying? What are their actions truly communicating? When your mentee makes poor choices on a constant basis, we must ask ourselves, "is there something deeper going on here?".

- What are the words under the words? Words are coming out of the mouth of your mentee, but what is really being said from the depths of their heart? It is the mature mentor that stops, asks the Lord what is truly going on, and speaks to the absence your mentee is experiencing. Instead of reacting to bad behavior (symptom), let us address the root of the problem (cause) with patience and grace.

Mentors often want to mentor because they could have used a mentor when they were a kid. "Be the mentor you wish you had" is a familiar saying. I have always been drawn to mentoring because I was a kid without much supervision who got into a lot of trouble. A lot of the things my mentee struggles with are the same things that I struggled with.

I am fortunate enough to have some perspective on the negative choices some of our mentees make. I have learned that there is usually more going on beneath the surface than I thought.

- Maybe your mentee sending you a million texts a day is more than just them seeking attention.

- Perhaps them doing whatever they have to do to get noticed is more than just "kids being kids".

- Maybe staying with their boyfriend/girlfriend, even when they don't like them, is a cry for help instead of a bad decision.

I have found that there is always a reason why a kid acts the way that they do. And more times than not, there is a need behind the deed.

When I would act like a fool in class, it wasn't because I wanted to be a jerk to my teacher. It was because I so badly wanted attention that I would do anything to get it. I would do whatever people said was cool, not because I necessarily liked it, but because I wanted so desperately to be liked and accepted. The deed might have been doing drugs or getting drunk, but the need was to forget about how hard life was, if only for a moment.

There is always a reason why a person acts the way they do. It is up to us as mentors, as mature adults who love and follow Jesus, to figure out the why behind the actions of our kids. When you figure out the why, compassion replaces judgment. Remember there is no such thing as a bad kid; only a hurt kid.

Over time, children will drop little clues as to the *why* behind their behavior. We must be on the lookout for those chances to invite and encourage them to share more by asking follow-up questions, one at a time. From there, it is up to them if they want to share or not. Just as the Lord does with us, we as mentors can only invite and then wait for a child to reply when they are ready. This cannot be forced.

All of us have basic needs that need to be met—needs like attention, acceptance, and approval. We all desire respect, security, and affection. For some of our mentees, they have no healthy way of getting those basic needs met. That is often the reason why they act in negative ways. You'd be amazed what a person will do to get their needs met, especially if they come from an unhealthy environment.

Before you judge the actions of your mentee, or get on to them for making poor choices, get curious and ask yourself the question, "What's the need behind the deed here?" And be sure to remember that there is always a reason why a child acts the way that they do—and that reason is less nefarious than you might initially think.

WHAT IS SUCCESS?

15

PROBLEM:

It is easy to feel ineffective and discouraged as a mentor when your mentee doesn't make the progress that you want them to make in the time frame that you have set for them.

PRINCIPLE:

Success in the eyes of the Lord is different than in the eyes of man, and we must focus more on their relationship with Jesus than on their earthly success.

PASSAGE:

"'For my thoughts are not your thoughts, neither are your ways my ways,' declares the Lord. 'As the heavens are higher than the earth, so are my ways higher than your ways and my thoughts than your thoughts.'" (Isaiah 55:8-9)

PRACTICE:

- Shift your thinking from celebrating the things you can see to celebrating the things you cannot see. Let your belief that your mentee's identity as a beloved child of God trump any success they may have in the world.

- Release your definition of success to the Lord and take up Jesus's definition of success. Seeing your mentee from Jesus' perspective means spending time with Jesus to get His eyes for your mentee.

- Remind yourself often. In the old testament, people created monuments to give them a visual reminder of God's care for them. They did this because people naturally forget. How can you remind yourself of true success on a consistent basis?

love to know what success looks like in any endeavor I take on.

At work, what are the goals I have to hit to be the best employee I can be?

At home, what grades do we want our kids to make and what college do we want them to attend?

You get the point.

For most of us mentors, one of the first things we want to know before we start mentoring is, "What does it mean to be a successful mentor?"

For a long time, I thought being a successful mentor meant behavior modification. I thought it was getting my mentee to act right and make good choices. And while a mentee maturing in behavior and decision making is a good thing, it is not the main thing.

Ephesians 5:1-2 says, "Therefore be imitators of God, as beloved children. And walk in love, as Christ loved us and gave himself up for us, a fragrant offering and sacrifice to God."

Success as a mentor means helping your mentee know that they are a beloved child of God. You do that by imitating God and loving your mentee with the unconditional love of Christ. It means connecting with them at a heart level and giving them someone they can trust.

Success as a mentor has has nothing to do with how much you know

It's not about how cool you are.

It's got nothing to do with your job title or how much money you make.

It's about giving them an example of Jesus and making them feel a part of His family.

The world puts labels on our kids.

They say they are worthless. Have no future. That there is something wrong with them.

But Jesus says otherwise, and it's our job as a mentor to help them know the truth.

Success as a mentor is making your mentee feel like they are full of worth.

It means making them feel like they are valuable and have something to offer.

It is helping them see themselves how God sees them.

A successful mentor helps their mentee believe that they are a child of God who has the love and affection of the Good & Perfect Father. That they have a spot at their Father's table and that He is for them, not against them.

It's hard not to love someone when you are speaking powerful words about how the Father sees them. Speaking identity over your mentee is a great way to let them know that you care. It will encourage them, motivate them, and boost their self-esteem and self-confidence.

Once that happens, I promise you that your mentee will be much more open to whatever skills you have to teach them. Then you can do what 2 Timothy 2:2 instructs, "And the things you have heard me say in the presence of many witnesses entrust to reliable people who will also be qualified to teach others."

There are a lot of important things a mentor can teach their mentee, but success as a mentor is about one thing: solidifying their identity as a child of God. To help them see themselves as God sees them. You cannot hit a target that does not exist. Our target, as mentors, is less about grades, cultural metrics, or behavior alteration and more about reaffirming the child's identity in Jesus. Make this your aim, and all else may follow.

A MENTOR'S JOB DESCRIPTION

16

PROBLEM:

Without a clear definition, Christian mentors often lack clarity about their role and responsibilities, leading to ambiguity around what success looks like and what they are accountable for.

PRINCIPLE:

The job of a Christian mentor is to make a disciple and to fulfill your mentee's potential. The best way to do that is to show up, build up, and share Jesus.

PASSAGE:

"Therefore go and make disciples of all nations, baptizing them in the name of the Father and of the Son and of the Holy Spirit, and teaching them to obey everything I have commanded you. And surely I am with you always, to the very end of the age." - Matthew 28:19-20

PRACTICE:

- Kids will experience Jesus as they experience you.

- Support and guide your mentee by teaching practical skills while also helping them navigate the emotional, mental, and relational challenges of life.

- Show up often in the life of your mentee to make them feel valued and important.

- Build up often with words of encouragement and by speaking the truth in love.

- Share Jesus with your mentee by teaching them about Christ and by embodying His character in your own life.

L et me start off with a question:

All of us are here today because of our relationship with *that person*. You know, the one who made a profound impact on your life. For me, a few men made me who I am today.

There was a man named Bob who invested in me when I was in college and helped me see my need for Jesus. There was a man named John who discipled me and taught me how to read the Scriptures. And there was a man named Steve who showed me the father-heart of God and helped me overcome my fatherless past.

Who got you to where you are today? Who invested in you?

Whether it was a parent, professor, coach, or someone else, all of us are who we are today because of the investment of others.

Now, you are here to learn how to invest in someone else. You could be *that person* for your future mentee.

Today, millions of kids need a positive adult to walk alongside them, to support and love them. Some are facing incredibly tough challenges like fatherlessness, poverty, and abuse. Others simply need someone to comfort them during hard times and to help them back up when they fall.

We all need encouragement. And that's why you're here today... to be a mentor who supports and encourages. One of the first things you need to know is the definition of a Christian mentor.

We believe a Christian mentor does two things: they make a disciple and fulfill their mentee's potential. Let's unpack that.

TO MAKE A DISCIPLE

"Follow me as I follow Christ." - 1 Corinthians 11:1

A disciple is a follower. You follow Christ, and your mentee gets the opportunity to follow you.

Kids will experience Jesus as they experience you. What an amazing opportunity to show them the love of Christ through your relationship. You get to teach them with your words and show them with your actions what it means to follow Jesus.

The Bible tells us to love God, love others, and make disciples. You already love God. Mentoring is a powerful way to love others. And you have the joy of discipling your mentee by creating a relationship built on trust, grace, and truth.

TO FULFILL POTENTIAL

"Train up a child in the way he should go; even when he is old he will not depart from it." Proverbs 22:6

We want to be a steady support and guide as our mentees grow and mature. Our desire is to offer wisdom and instruction when they face obstacles on their journey. As they trek down the path of life, we're on the sidelines cheering them on.

We have the opportunity to teach practical skills, but also to walk with them through the emotional, mental, and relational twists and turns of life.

We want our mentees to walk in the fullness of who God created them to be. We want them to flourish in every area of life.

That's what Christian mentoring is all about: helping fulfill your mentee's potential while consistently showing and sharing the person of Jesus Christ.

So now that you know what a Christian mentor *is*, what exactly does a mentor *do*?

Being a mentor is all about building relationships, because we believe that relationships change lives. Sermons and books are helpful. Podcasts and websites can teach you something. But God has always used people to bring others closer to Him.

That's why Jesus came to earth and spent his public ministry years with just twelve people. There are many fun and creative ways to build relationships, but there are three things that must form the foundation of every effective Christian mentoring relationship.

We call this a mentor's job description:

SHOW UP

Showing up is the most important thing you can do as a mentor. How do you build any successful relationship? You spend time with that person. You learn new things about them and you experience life with them. You make them feel important. You make them feel valued. You make them feel like you matter. And you do that by showing up.

BUILD UP

Our desire is for our mentors to speak truth into the lives of our mentees. We want our mentors to encourage them with every word that comes out of their mouth. Our words matter. Our tone matters. Our facial expressions and body language matter. We want our mentees to know that we are for them, no matter what.

SHARE JESUS

As a mentor, you can't give what you don't have. More than anything, we want our mentees to love Jesus Christ with all their hearts. They'll learn how to do that by watching you, listening to you, and spending time with you.

We're not here just to produce good men or good women. We're here to help raise up followers of Christ. So remember: the impact you make isn't about how much you know or how perfectly you perform. It's about showing up, building up, and pointing your mentee to the One who changes everything.

Because in the end, the best gift you can give your mentee is not your wisdom, your skills, or your time. The best gift you can give is *you*, surrendered to Jesus. And God will do the rest.

DISCUSSION QUESTIONS:

- What part of the mentor's "job description" (show up, build up, share Jesus) do you feel most confident in? Which part challenges you most?

- What might be holding you back from more openly sharing your faith with your mentee?

- What are some signs that your mentoring is making a difference—even if they're small?

- In what areas do you need to release control and trust that God is working even when you don't see immediate results?

ALL FRUSTRATION COMES FROM UNMET EXPECTATIONS

17

PROBLEM:

Due to human nature, mentors can unknowingly create expectations for mentees that are unspoken, unfair, and even unattainable.

PRINCIPLE:

The best mentors shelve their personal desires for their mentee and focus on doing whatever they can to help their mentee's goals, dreams, and aspirations come to fruition.

PASSAGE:

"Do nothing out of selfish ambition or vain conceit. Rather, in humility value others above yourselves, not looking to your own interests but each of you to the interests of the others." (Philippians 2:3-4)

PRACTICE:

- Rid yourself of the expectations you put on your mentee. Focus on what you can control and let go of what you cannot. Trust the Lord will move in His perfect timing.

- Ask more questions. Make it commonplace to ask your mentee about what they want in life and create action steps to help them achieve their goals. Get good at asking questions to help draw out the desires from the heart of your mentee.

- Give less directives. Make sure you are not unknowingly placing your own personal expectations or desires on the shoulders of your mentee.

- Be flexible in your mentoring relationship. It's not about what you want, but about what your mentee wants and what the Lord wants.

There is a temptation in mentoring to try to get your mentee to emulate all that worked for you. You want your mentee to go to college, get a job, wear a suit, and get married because you went to college, got a job, wore a suit, and got married. But what if your mentee doesn't want to go to college? What if instead of a suit and high-and-tight haircut, he prefers baggy jeans and dreadlocks? Will you be disappointed?

A saying that rings true especially when mentoring kids from hard places is, "All frustration comes from unmet expectations." I know for me, I had unspoken expectations that I placed on my mentee without even knowing it.

I expected them to make good grades, to be polite, and to have athletic success. I wanted them to dress a certain way, speak a certain way, and go to church.

Don't get me wrong, these are all good things. There is nothing wrong with giving your mentee the option to do as you have done. But your way is one way, it is not *the* way. We must be careful not to get caught up trying to get them to emulate us instead of Christ. We want people to be shaped into God's image, not the image of our own personal history.

I know for me, when my mentees desires didn't line up with my desires for them, it caused frustration in our relationship. I could not understand why they wanted something different than what I wanted for them. It would cause me to judge them unfairly which placed a rift in our relationship.

Your mentee is different from you. He or she has a different story, different skills, and a personality that may not look like yours. Work with your mentee to figure out what God's unique, individual call and plan is for him or her.

The first step is letting go of the expectations you have for your mentee. As hard as it may be, don't focus on the end results. Instead, focus on the process of showing up and loving them right where they are. Love them right where they are and accept them just as they are, instead of getting on to them because they are not where you think they should be.

When our expectations aren't met, frustration sets in. When negativity enters your relationship, the enemy uses it to wreak havoc on the trust you've built together. It's okay to hope your mentee goes to college or has athletic success, but don't expect it. Expectation is rigid, but hope is flexible. Expectation is assuming something will happen. Hope is wishing or desiring good to happen. Don't bury your mentee with the weight of having to live up to your expectations.

We all have dreams for our mentees, and there is nothing wrong with that. But a question to ask your mentee is "What are your dreams?" Once you know what they want, you can focus on making their dreams come true, instead of the dreams that you want for them.

EARN THE RIGHT
TO BE HEARD

18

PROBLEM:

Mentors expect mentees to listen and heed their instruction because of their seniority and experience.

PRINCIPLE:

Mentees will listen to their mentor only after trust is built and the mentor has proved that they have the mentee's best interest in mind.

PASSAGE:

"Consider it pure joy, my brothers and sisters, whenever you face trials of many kinds, because you know that the testing of your faith produces perseverance. Let perseverance finish its work so that you may be mature and complete, not lacking anything." (James 1:2-4)

PRACTICE:

- Make Deposits. We must make deposits in the life of our mentee before we can make a withdrawal. Deposits include doing what you say you will do and proving to your mentee that you can be counted on for support regardless of circumstances.

- Stay in the Game. Patience and perseverance is needed, as the length of time it takes to earn the right to be heard differs depending on your mentee.

- Consistency is king. You have to remain consistent and continue to deposit good things into the life of your mentee, trusting those deposits will produce a mentee who trusts you, will listen to you, and who will open up to you.

You may have heard the saying from John Maxwell that "a kid doesn't care what you know until they know that you care." It is one of my favorite quotes because it is 100% accurate.

I have seen many mentors get rejected when they try to start the mentoring relationship by giving the mentee advice. Simply put, your mentee really doesn't care what you know. Most are not impressed by your job title or college degree. They don't want to hear about your financial planning strategy or how you became successful—at least not right off the bat.

We must earn the right to be heard.

Early on in my mentoring journey, one of my mentees named Jason wanted nothing to do with me. All I got from him were icy glares, one word answers, and sarcastic put downs. I would come home rejected and thinking that Jason hated me. This was a "trial" in my mentoring journey.

But it was just a test. You see, while I thought Jason didn't like me, he was really sizing me up to see if he would allow me to be a part of his life. He wasn't being mean; he was protecting himself. Jason didn't open up until he knew that I was the real deal, and that took a lot of work. I had to pass the test before he allowed me to enter into his life, and that took a great deal of perseverance.

Here are three ways that you can earn the right to be heard with your mentee.

1. Keep showing up. Perseverance is required in your mentoring journey. Some mentees will warm up to you the second they meet you, but others, especially older mentees, may take some time. You can win their hearts by continuing to show up time after time with a smile on your face. Know that the fight for their heart is worth it, and the waiting will pay dividends as your relationship progresses. Sarcasm, impatience, or a failure to understand why they won't open up will delay progress. Smiles, asking questions, and putting yourself in their shoes will help open up the door.

2. Seek first to understand. Realize that asking your mentee to open up to a total stranger is a tall order. Entering into the relationship with humility is a great way to earn you the right to be heard. You don't know what your mentee has been through nor their personality or temperament. They may have been burned by opening up in the past and you will have to labor to bandage those wounds and create trust. Spend the first season of your mentoring relationship seeking to understand who they are and where they come from. Make it your mission to learn as much as you possibly can about your mentee and how they are wired. As opportunities arise, open them up to your life and model vulnerability.

3. Make their life better. Serving your mentee in whatever way necessary is a great way to earn the right to be heard. How can you make their life better? Be on the lookout for creative ways to bless them. Maybe they need a ride somewhere or a connection to get a job? Perhaps it's giving them access to a new experience or a place to hang out with their friends. It could be

as simple as encouraging them and making sure they leave your presence with a laugh and a smile. Serving them in practical and encouraging ways is a great way to earn favor with your mentee. After all, it's difficult to stay cold and short with someone who has bent over backwards to improve your life.

Some mentees give you their trust right away, while others wait for a long time. All of this depends on a variety of factors, including age, past experiences, and personality. If your mentee seems like they have put up a wall or don't want anything to do with you, just wait. Sooner or later they will warm up to you. Don't take offense. When we take things personally we are not earning the right to be heard but stifling our influence altogether. See the difficulty as a challenge by saying, "I'll show up and love this kid no matter how they treat me."

CREATING A SAFE ENVIRONMENT

19

PROBLEM:

Mentors who do not come from traumatic circumstances struggle to comprehend the need for a safe environment and do not intentionally prioritize creating one.

PRINCIPLE:

A safe environment with a foundation of trust, unconditional love, and acceptance is the essential ingredient needed to help your mentee flourish.

PASSAGE:

"There is no fear in love, but perfect love casts out fear. For fear has to do with punishment, and whoever fears has not been perfected in love." (1 John 4:18)

PRACTICE:

- React well. Regardless of what your mentee does or says, try not to overreact. Even if you are panicking on the inside, let us react with calmness and love.

- It's not what you say, but *how* you say it. Be aware of your non-verbal communication, especially your tone, body language, and volume.

- Exude peace and stability. In a world that is full of chaos and instability, be the rock in your mentee's life. May they know that they can count on you to be a peaceful and stable presence who is always there for them.

Trust is the foundation of your mentoring relationship. Above all else, your mentee has to believe that you are good and that you want them to succeed.

The author Stephen Covey says, "Trust is the glue of life. It's the most essential ingredient in effective communication. It's the foundational principle that holds all relationships."

But what if your mentee has experienced hard times? What if there is trauma in their past or they have been betrayed by those who should have been taking care of them?

Because of their histories, it is often difficult for these children to trust the loving adults in their lives, which often results in perplexing behaviors.

While a variety of mentoring strategies may be successful with some children, children with histories of harm need caregiving that meets their unique needs and addresses the whole child.

That is why even some of the most successful parents are confused when what worked with their child does not work with their mentee.

Trust must be established between the mentor and the mentee before you can take any steps of progress in your mentoring relationship. And it can take some time. The reality is that some mentees trust their mentor in three weeks while it takes others over a year. But we can't give up. We must continue to show up to build trust.

Our mentees have to trust that you will love them in the good and the bad. They must be certain that you will not unexpectedly abandon them or hurt them in any way.

Trust is solidified by replacing judgment with compassion and speaking to them in an honoring way.

The best way to build trust is to create a safe environment. Here's how:

- Get down on their level.

- Make eye contact with them.

- Give them space and go at their pace.

- Smile often.

- Give appropriate touch.

- Use words of affirmation often.

- Provide undivided attention.

- Be patient.

When your mentee raises their emotions, you stay calm. Listen to them.

This works with eight year olds and eighteen year olds. Even if they look like grown adults, we must always remember that they are still children on the inside.

This safe environment will create a nurturing relationship built on a foundation of trust.

For some of our kids, they are used to adults telling them all that they are doing wrong. Some rarely see an adult smile and take time out of their day to notice them. You get to be the exception.

Keep showing up with a smile. Create a safe environment. Be a stable, consistent adult that they can count on. If your mentee lives in a world where chaos and instability is their normal, meet them with peace and stability.

AM I QUALIFIED?

20

PROBLEM:

Too many mentors walk in insecurity or pass on the opportunity to invest in the lives of young people because they falsely believe they are underqualified for the role.

PRINCIPLE:

God can use anyone to transform a life. Mentoring is sharing your imperfect life with your mentee, not about having all the answers. It's about entering into someone else's world and inviting them into yours.

PASSAGE:

"He who calls you is faithful; he will surely do it." (1 Thessalonians 5:24)

PRACTICE:

- Build yourself up. Set aside the time for the Lord to calm your insecurities and to believe that He who called you is faithful (see 1 Thessalonians 5:24).

- Focus on faith. Faith is needed to walk out in your assignment as a mentee, so do whatever you have to do to stir up your faith on a continual basis.

- Protect yourself. Reject the lies that the enemy peppers you with and lean into the truth that God makes good on His word.

When people consider starting a mentoring relationship with a child, one question that seems to always pop up is "Am I qualified?"

After all, investing into the life of a child is a big deal.

And I get it. Oftentimes I wonder if I myself am qualified to be a mentor. What happens if I have a bad couple weeks and feel totally ill-equipped to have someone follow my actions? Perhaps I take a hit at work or my marriage is struggling. Does that disqualify me? Would God want me to mentor if I haven't kept up with my Bible reading plan or if I have missed small group for the last four weeks?

But I think we are asking the wrong question. Instead of asking "Am I qualified?", start asking "Am I a couple steps ahead of my mentee?"

If you are, then you have something to offer.

Healthy mentors show mentees every part of their lives— the good and the bad. Mentees should have a front row seat to seeing how a Christian handles everything that this world throws at them. This takes a large amount of courage and humility.

John Maxwell said, "If you want to impress people, tell them about your successes. If you want to impact people, tell them about your failures."

All of us are a work in progress. The goal is not perfection or having it all figured out. The goal is to become more like Jesus.

I hope you are learning new things in all areas of your life: professionally, physically, relationally, and most importantly, *spiritually*.

1 Corinthians 11:1 says, "Follow my example, as I follow the example of Christ."

As a a mentor, following the example of Christ looks like this:

- He loved unconditionally

- He forgave his enemies

- He accepted people, just like they were

- He spend time with God the Father

- He pursued the things of God instead of the things of this world

So are you a couple steps ahead of your mentee in life? Are you doing your best to follow Christ? Are you willing to allow your mentee into your life and give them an example to follow?

If the answer to all of those questions is "yes", then I believe you are qualified to mentor. And I am confident that the Lord can use you to positively impact the life of a child. Because the Lord loves to use the most unassuming characters to do His work.

Moses was given up at birth and murdered a man.

David was an overlooked shepherd boy.

Mary Magdalene had a demon and Paul persecuted Christians.

All were used mightily by God.

If God can use them, then he can surely use you.

Focus on the one who calls you instead of on your own resume, personal accolades, or accomplishments. Dial in on serving your mentee and loving them unconditionally. If you take your eyes off yourself and respond to the call with faith, you'll be exactly what your mentee needs.

FAITHFULNESS OVER FRUITFULNESS

21

PROBLEM:

Mentors gauge their effectiveness and worth through the achievements and worldly success of their mentee.

PRINCIPLE:

While seeing your mentee have success is of some value, mentors must focus on their words and actions instead of their mentee's wins and accomplishments.

PASSAGE:

"I planted the seed, Apollos watered it, but God has been making it grow. So neither the one who plants nor the one who waters is anything, but only God, who makes things grow." (1 Corinthians 3:6-7)

PRACTICE:

- Remember who is in control: the Lord is and we are not. Focus on what you can control instead of fretting about what you can't control.

- Our job is to be faithful. His job is to produce the fruit. Yes, we show up with our watering can in hand, but we always trust God to grow the fruit.

- There are indicators of success and we should celebrate those, but we don't rely on them to prove our worth as mentors.

Early on in my mentoring journey, I thought mentoring was like a math equation.

A + B = C

If I showed up + gave them some wisdom = I would see growth in my mentee, right?

If I'm being honest, in my naivete, I thought my mere presence would solve all of my mentees issues.

I thought, because of me, my mentee would improve academically and grow spiritually. It was only a matter of time before they became their best self.

But what happened when my mentee didn't grow as fast as I thought they should? How would bad grades or negative behaviors affect our relationship? How would I respond when my mentee didn't seem to care about what I had to say?

My friends Kyle and Mary mentored twelve kids when they were first married. They started with a group of young men when they were in junior high and continued to meet with them every Sunday until they graduated high school.

For years, they invested a ton into these young men, and the young men were extremely grateful for their hospitality, wisdom, and guidance. Except for one young man.

Eleven of the boys said thank you every week. One did not.

Eleven of the boys said the group changed their life. One did not.

Eleven of the boys grew academically and spiritually. One did not.

When the group came to an end, Kyle and Mary looked at each other and said, "We sure did make a difference in eleven of the boys' lives. Too bad we couldn't reach that one boy."

Fast forward about 20 years and Kyle is filling up with gas one afternoon. He sees a random man in his late thirties approaching. He leans up against Kyle's car and says, "Excuse me. Is your name Kyle?"

"Yes. Can I help you?" Kyle responded.

"You probably don't remember me, but I just wanted to say *thank you*. I sat in your house every Sunday night for years and didn't say a word. I'm now a husband and a father and everything I know about leading my family I learned by being in your small group. I couldn't say it then, but here I am to say it now: *Thank you*."

And he walked off.

It was that one young man whom they thought just didn't get it.

For decades, my friends thought that they had missed it with that young man. Because they focused on the fruit and what they could see in him, they thought they had failed. But the Lord had other plans.

Here's the lesson: so often in mentoring, we want to focus on the fruit of our efforts with our mentee. As a result, when the fruit doesn't come, we can get discouraged. And when we get discouraged, we don't show up as often and we even consider quitting.

We all want to see fruit like maturity, good grades, vibrant faith, and good decision making. Your mentee may rapidly improve and you may see fruit. Or, just like the kid in Kyle's story, you may not see any fruit and it may feel like a waste of time. But you never know what the Lord is doing underneath the hood. Oftentimes, more is happening than we think. Even after we leave the garden, God is working to grow the places that we have invested in.

FINISH WELL

22

PROBLEM:

Abruptly ending a mentoring relationship without a thoughtful plan in place can do a tremendous amount of damage to the heart of your mentee.

PRINCIPLE:

When the time comes to part ways with your mentee, develop an exit strategy to finish the relationship well to protect and care for the heart of your mentee.

PASSAGE:

"After Paul had finished speaking, he knelt down with all of them and prayed. Everyone cried and hugged and kissed him.They were especially sad because Paul had told them, 'You will never see me again.' Then they went with him to the ship." (Acts 20:36-38)

PRACTICE:

- Have a plan. When you realize the end of the relationship is near, formulate a plan to finish well with your mentee.

- Celebrate Good Times. Facilitate closure in a healthy way by clearly communicating the ending while celebrating what the Lord did in your relationship.

- Who's on Deck? Comb through your network to set your mentee up for future relationships. The best mentors never drop their mentee, they simply hand them over to a trusted friend for the next stage of their journey.

What do you do whenever major life circumstances pop up that get in the way of your mentoring relationship?

Maybe your mentee goes off to college or moves to a new community?

Perhaps you get a new job and have to move across town or to another state?

What if you started mentoring when you were single, but now have a family with a bunch of little kids running around?

Whatever the case may be, the reality is there will probably come a day when your mentoring relationship ends. When this happens, finishing well and providing healthy closure is key in maintaining a positive outlook on the mentoring experience.

For me personally, I had a lot of mentors in my life, and anytime one would leave, I found myself taking it personally. This had nothing to do with my mentor, but everything to do with my past.

We must remember that our mentees are kids. Some have wounds, significant wounds, that haven't yet been healed. Grace has to abound with our mentees. You may do everything right, and they will still be hurt and mad at you. That's ok. You are strong and mature enough to absorb that.

Some of our mentees have been abandoned in the past, either by a family member or by another mentor. Kids who have been left are constantly looking for ways to avoid being hurt. They have a hard time believing the best and tend to assume the worst—with good reason I might add.

Them getting into a relationship in the first place takes a ridiculous amount of courage. That's the thing about relationships, they can be risky. Why? Because you have to give trust—trust that they will do good by you and not hurt you.

This is exactly why leaving can be so hard, but here are five things you can do to help leave in the healthiest way possible.

1. *Celebrate*. We suggest having some sort of event to celebrate your mentoring relationship. Invite everyone who was involved with the mentoring relationship, meaning your family, their family, and any mentoring organization who helped facilitate the connection. Talk about memories that you created and milestones that the mentee hit. Discuss all the good things that happened in your relationship.

2. *Network*. If the mentee has a desire to continue to be mentored, perhaps go through your network and see if anyone you know can take your place. You may be in a season where you don't have the margin to mentor, but what about your co-worker, neighbor, or family member? If the mentee and their family agree to the new mentor, you can help create a new match. Bonus points if the mentee already knows the new mentor and you can facilitate the exchange in person.

3. *Promises*. Be careful about making promises that you are not sure you can keep. We all know that we have the best of intentions, but we do not want to disappoint our mentees with unfulfilled promises. For instance, if you promise that after the transition you will call them once per quarter to check in, you must follow through.

If you tell them you will help them write a resume when they finish school in two years, don't dodge them when they reach out down the road. If you aren't absolutely sure you can follow through, don't make the promise to begin with.

4. *Communicate*. Even though you may not be formally mentoring your mentee anymore, that doesn't mean you cannot communicate with them. If you'd still like to stay connected to your mentee, find a time to talk and put it into your calendar. I know a mentor who called his former mentee every Sunday night at 8 pm for years. Especially as your mentee grows and matures, It truly is fun to watch them go from child to adult and mentee to peer.

5. *Affirm them.* Anytime someone leaves a mentee who has been left before, it can create an opportunity for the enemy to creep in and lie to them. For me, I would believe things like, "I did something wrong," "I'm un-lovable", or "This is always going to happen." If you get the sense that your mentee is feeling abandonment by your leaving, dispel those lies by stating the truth. Say things like, "You did nothing wrong and I still care for you," "You are lovable. This is more about me than you," or "People will come and go, but that doesn't mean they don't love you."

Ending a relationship, especially with a mentee who you have grown close to, will always be a tough deal. But you can facilitate closure in a healthy way by celebrating what the Lord did in your relationship and setting your mentee up for future mentoring relationships. All good things must come to an end, and mentoring is no different.

PARTNERING WITH PARENTS

23

PROBLEM:

Mentors can fail to realize the importance of including the parents or guardians in their relationship with their mentee.

PRINCIPLE:

Instead of siloing off and it being all about you, commit to including the parent or guardian in your mentoring journey. This will take more effort and time at the beginning, but the work in the early stages will most certainly provide a smoother ride in the end.

PASSAGE:

"Love must be sincere. Hate what is evil; cling to what is good. Be devoted to one another in love. Honor one another above yourselves." (Romans 12:9-10)

PRACTICE:

- *Set the tone.* From the get-go, we meet the parent, communicate with them and remain accessible to the parent.

- *Essential Worker.* We view the parent as an essential and integral part of the mentoring relationship and would be wise to invest into them, just as we invest into the mentee.

- *Culture of Honor.* Show honor to the parent for who they are and for their role in the life of your mentee—even if you don't always agree with their decisions.

When I was overseeing a mentoring organization, I unfortunately had the opportunity to see a few mentoring relationships fall apart. One day, a mentor came to me and said he had an argument with his mentee's parent about a small issue at school. The mentor didn't agree with the parent and let her know about it in a very straightforward way.

The mom asked for a new mentor a week later.

Regardless of whether or not you agree with the parenting tactics of your mentee's guardian, you must always remember that they will always be in charge of your mentee. It is their child.

Think of it this way: Who is your mentee going to listen to? Their family member who they've known their whole life, or you whom they just met?

You're going to lose that battle every time.

That is why partnering with your mentee's guardian is one of the best moves you can make as a mentor. When the guardian and the mentor are on the same team, that creates the best possible outcome for the mentee. When the guardian has your back, that only helps your relationship with your mentee.

When I began mentoring, I made the mistake of dismissing the mother of my mentee. My actions said, "I'm here for the kid and your presence is only getting in the way." That made my mentoring relationship significantly more difficult than it had to be.

The most important person in your mentee's life is their

parent/guardian. Building a relationship with them is a great way to show honor, respect, and kindness.

Mentors value the mentee's family by:

- Communicating regularly

- Always giving as much information about activities and scheduled events as possible to their parent/guardian

- Expressing thankfulness for being trusted to be a part of their child's life

- Looking for opportunities to love and serve the family

- Praying for them

We've had a few younger mentees who weren't thrilled with being paired up with a mentor. If mom took the side of the mentor, it was only a matter of time before that mentee changed his attitude. If the parent is on board, the kid usually follows.

On the other hand, if the parent somehow turns against the mentor or the mentoring organization, that usually means the end of the mentoring relationship is near. If the parent is not on board, the kid usually follows.

I know you may not have signed up to build a relationship with your mentee's family, but it comes with the territory. What a great opportunity to get to know a new family, and to introduce them to your world as well. Have them over for dinner, go to their events, or invite them to church. This is an easy way to "love thy neighbor".

Here are some things to avoid:

- Never talk bad or dishonor a member of your mentee's family, even if the mentee is doing it. Always honor them with your words, no matter what they have done. Remember you are talking to a child, and you never want to create animosity between a child and a parent, even if that parent is making poor choices. You don't have to agree with the parent or even condone what they are doing, but you do have to show respect and honor.

- Avoid judging the family or telling the mentee that they are out of line.

- Do not voluntarily give advice to the parent/guardian, unless they initiate it.

Occasionally, you will disagree with your mentee's guardians. If this happens, you must ask yourself if the issue is big enough to address. You must be wise in picking your battles. If you are in doubt, ask your mentoring organization or your community for insight. Obviously any situation where your mentee is in danger is an automatic issue to confront, but other times may not be so black and white.

If you do choose to confront the issue, please do so with humility and kindness, as a guardian can be naturally defensive when discussing parenting tactics.

When the family of your mentee flourishes, your mentee flourishes. When they struggle, it rubs off on the mentee. If you really want the best for your mentee, to include the family and do whatever you can to help them succeed as well.

HOPE DEALER

24

PROBLEM:

Our mentees can easily begin to lose a sense of hope for tomorrow without a clear and distinct purpose today.

PRINCIPLE:

Your mentee thinks about their future often. If they are living in a hard home or school situation, they will struggle to have hope of a healthy future too. Mentors have the power to speak into this issue and offer purpose and hope.

PASSAGE:

"Faith is the reality of what we hope for, the proof of what we don't see." (Hebrews 11:1)

PRACTICE:

- Be the Constant. You will have bad days. You are human. However, as you prepare to hang out with your mentee, pray for the Lord to free you of what is bugging you in the moment and anoint your time with your mentee. Pray for His strength to forget your worries and wear a smile as your mentee sits down and makes eye contact with you.

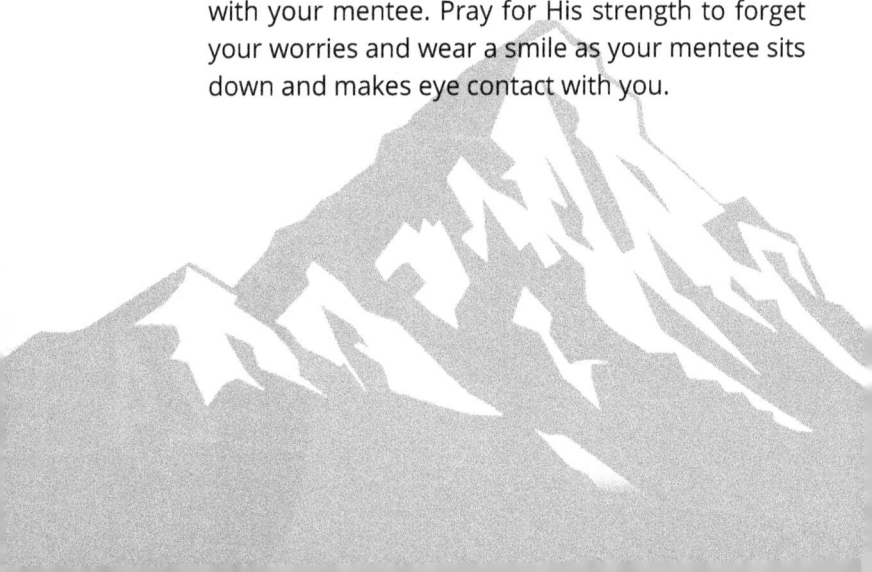

An old analogy used to describe the power of hope involves a prison yard. For a guard to break the spirit of a prisoner, all he must do is start by having him spend an entire day moving an enormous pile of rocks from one area of the yard to another on Monday. While the prisoner may be dehydrated and exhausted, barely even able to walk or think straight, he can at least look back on the day's work with some sense of pride and accomplishment. Then on Tuesday, the guard forces the prisoner to put all the rocks back in their original place. He repeats the process for as many days as it takes for the prisoner to realize his hard work is pointless and without purpose.

Now, some of us feel the same way about the never-ending hopelessness of doing laundry or making our beds each morning! The truth regarding our mentee is that without a clear and distinct purpose, they can easily begin to lose a sense of hope for the future. Your mentee is thinking about the future all the time. If they are living in a hard home or school situation, you can bet they struggle to have hope of a healthy future too.

This is where the mentor steps in and adds the much-needed consistency and positivity the mentee needs to know that "this too shall pass."

Hope, by definition, is the ability to rise above our circumstances to know that even though things are at their worst or darkest, there will come a time that the light will pierce the darkness and peace and prosperity will return. Even with a strong sense of identity, an unexercised purpose leaves us wanting.

Your mentee may have a great head on her shoulders and feel confident in who she is. The problem can be she doesn't have the all-important framework of intentionality and motivation to help her develop her purpose. I would run into this issue often while working with teenagers in our youth group. There's nothing harder for one's faith than when they realize they are the strongest Christian they know. I can remember empathizing with individual teenagers who were head and shoulders above all their peers when it came to the seriousness of their faith. It's a tough place to be when the only way you feel you can go is down.

When you have your mentee take stock of their lives and environment only to discover they are surrounded by unhealthy relationships in their homes and friendship circles, it's all the more reason to offer hope as a mentor.

So how do we instill a healthy hope into the hearts of our mentees? Your consistency will speak volumes to your mentee as they most likely have very little at home and in their friend group they can count on.

Of all the things they can be known for, Christians should be characterized by their practice of prayer and their unfazed priority of hope. The writer of Hebrews tells us that our faith is being sure of what we hope for and certain of what we can't see. It's realizing that God is in the constant work of connecting and reconnecting His creation in many ways.

It is incredible that we get the chance, through mentoring, to listen to the cares of our mentees, to pray for their issues, and, with the Spirit leading, to offer truth and encouragement!

Work hard daily to be the constant in your mentee's life. You will have bad days. You will struggle to always be hopeful. However, make it a point to have yourself prepared before each meeting with your mentee. Make it a ritual that as you walk up those school steps and open that front door to head to check in at the office, you pray for the Lord to free you of what is bugging you in the moment and anoint your time with your mentee. Pray for His strength to forget your worries and wear a smile as your mentee sits down and makes eye contact with you.

Hope is intentional, so come prepared. Did you come across an article that might speak hope to your mentee's situation? Come ready to share it. Do you have an anecdote of another youth who was in the same struggle as your mentee but is now thriving? Offer the story. Hope is not a wish or a fleeting fantasy. It is a genuine force that can be grabbed and shared—so do it with intentionality.

THE DOCTRINE OF MARGIN

25

PROBLEM:

Margin is a foreign concept for many mentors as their mentality and lifestyle is to survive instead of thrive.

PRINCIPLE:

Healthy mentors commit to creating and cultivating margin in their daily lives. They are then free to operate out of this margin which allows for balanced and calm reactions and wise instruction and encouragement.

PASSAGE:

"Come to me, all you who are weary and burdened, and I will give you rest. Take my yoke upon you and learn from me, for I am gentle and humble in heart, and you will find rest for your souls." (Matthew 11:28-29)

PRACTICE:

- Be intentional. Remember that you control your schedule, it does not control you!

- Learn to say, "No, thank you." I get it, you're a sweet person and you wish you could help everyone in need. However, there aren't enough hours in the day. When asked to do yet another thing from someone, tell them you will take some time, pray about the need, and check to make sure it works with your schedule.

- Define and defend your boundaries. Taking up for your emotional and mental health is not selfish, it's smart! Life is a marathon and not a sprint. We want to make sure we are pacing ourselves and not quickly burning out.

- Simplify! Sometimes less can be so much more. You know that great feeling when you tidy up your closet or garage? You can do that mentally by looking at your weekly or monthly calendar and prioritizing your activities. Cut out what needs to go!

- Carve out margins in your day. Take some time each day for prayer, quiet, and enjoyment. By the way...sabbath: ever heard of it!? God intended that you actually practice a day each week to rest and enjoy His presence undistracted!

One of the best things our mentees can learn from us is the doctrine of margin. Do you remember when we were first introduced to "margins" on lined notebook paper. If you were like me, you were taught to keep your work within the margins. They were to be our starting point and ending point for all the words and numbers we would fill our assignments with. The margins were important because they gave our teachers space to make corrections and leave notes—room for correcting and learning.

The older I get, the more I see the need for creating and cultivating margins in our lives. Without margin, we are prone to focusing on *surviving* on a basic level as opposed to *thriving* at a higher one. Think of it this way: margins are the excess. Some people have excess money, so they can be generous with giving some to others. Some have time, so they can spend it investing in others by calling them, visiting them, sitting with them to hear about their day and offer advice when it's needed.

Let me be brutally honest about margin: no one cares if you have any. The real issue with margin is you don't "need" it to function. What that really means is that a lot of people are living their entire lives each day at an emotional, mental, physical, and spiritual breaking point. And, sadly, these people do not prioritize margin in others because they have no idea of how to build it and function out of it in their own lives.

I had an epiphany about margin about a decade into full-time church leadership. One Sunday morning a personnel committee member asked if he could meet with me in my office later in the week. When Marcus arrived at the church office, I was frantically making last minute preparations for an upcoming trip and, I'll admit, I was a little nervous about the meeting wondering if it was called because I had done something wrong.

Marcus sat patiently across from me as I finished up a call and made some notes before swinging my office chair back in his direction to give him my undivided attention. He asked if he could pray for me and as he did, I fought the urge to answer the office phone as it rang.

After the amens, Marcus asked a curious question. He said, "Are you making sure to take your day off each week away from this building and away from your phone?" The question hit like a lightning bolt. The funny thing was that up until that point, I always had people making it their job to make sure I was doing mine. While every senior pastor and committee member was adamant about the days I was on, Marcus was the first person to ask about my day off.

He had been a staff member of a "successful" mega church that had a track record for high-speed growth. What I didn't know before that day was that Marcus' story included losing his job (and family) because of improprieties stemming from his inability to deal with the pressures of high output results. Marcus blessed me as a mentor from that day on. He always made it a point to make sure I was practicing Sabbath and getting as much out of my one day off as I was giving during my six days on.

Creating margin first means taking stock in how much you have already. How would you rate your emotional, physical, or financial margin? Are you operating out of a thriving life right now or are you merely surviving? If you were to get some bad news or go through a trial, would you be able to remain healthy and focused or would it shut down your life?

Do you have any disposable resources right now? Is anything going unused as far as your weekly schedule, your bank account, or your storage facility out on the highway? Could you add an hour-long meeting to your weekly schedule or are you booked solid? Is there room in your finances to donate $50 a month to your favorite nonprofit? If you have no margin of time right now, is there any part of your week that you could sacrifice to make yourself available to volunteer?

Another important thing to remember when it comes to margin is that many of us feel like we don't have any because of life doing it to us. I challenge that thinking. I believe we make the choice to fill up our schedules. It's not that we don't have time; it's that we have filled our time with what we think matters most. A constant evaluating of our priorities will help us feel less like the victim and more in control of the choices we make. When we interact with our mentees from a healthy place of margin we will find we have more to offer them and they have the confidence to offer more of themselves to us.

SAGE ON THE STAGE OR GUIDE ON THE SIDE?

26

PROBLEM:

Mentors are not fiery preachers behind a raised pulpit who judge as the ultimate authority and theological superior.

PRINCIPLE:

Healthy mentors carry the posture of one called to walk next to mentees (not lord over them) through life experiences.

PASSAGE:

"Two of Jesus' disciples were going to the village of Emmaus, which was about eleven kilometers from Jerusalem. As they were talking and thinking about what had happened, Jesus came near and started walking along beside them." (Luke 24:13-15)

PRACTICE:

- Listen to your mentee from a place of relatability and understanding. If you are tempted to minimize or reject your mentee's issues because they seem trite, remember that even small social issues are huge to a 14-year old.

- Put yourself in their shoes. Remember what life was like at their age. Those insecurities and worries are universal and transcendent. Rest assured it's no easier today than it was back then!

- Be a guide from the side! Speak from a place of wisdom and experience while talking to your mentee. Use "us" and "we" language.

- Avoid being sage from the stage. Your mentee does not need a tone-deaf and self-righteous sermon or bible verses taken out of context.

So, who grew up going to "big church"? Isn't that a funny term many of us grew up hearing and saying? For those that don't know, big church simply means the worship service that typically takes place after Sunday school or small group gatherings on Sunday mornings.

"Big church" is where the big guns come out in the form of the choir, the band or orchestra, and the weekly sermon presented by the senior pastor. As someone who was saved as a teenager, the big church culture was new to me. Park Place Baptist had the largest room I had ever been in (besides the Astrodome). Like, it was large enough to accommodate the Goodyear blimp if need be. And besides its size, it had ornate designs and architectural features behind the stage and on every wall. I must admit, I spent many an hour counting shapes and designs on the walls as my mind drifted and waned from staying up too late the night before as the pastor sermonized.

Speaking of the pastor, I always thought it was interesting how he stood behind a large wooden cabinet that mimicked a captain's wheel of a ship as he orated for 45 minutes from the Bible. He stood high above us and faced us directly, sometimes pointing down to us and occasionally hitting the surface of the pulpit to emphasize a truth. He was the sage on the stage.

The image of a pastor preaching from a regal pulpit is a good contrast for us as we consider the posture of the mentor. Like me, you probably learned the difference between authoritarian and authoritative leadership in school. The skinny of it is that an authoritarian leader gives commands and requires absolute obedience while the authoritative leader is one who highlights cooperation and discussion and desires to lead by setting an example. Authoritarians speak *at* people while an authoritative leader speaks *with* people.

How crazy would it be for your mentee to walk in on your next meeting together and see you standing behind a pulpit asking her to take a seat directly in front of you as you proceed to preach a message for 45 minutes and the only reply you allow from her is "amen!"? We as mentors should consider our role as authoritative leaders who have been called to walk *alongside* our mentees in life. We should not carry the posture of one facing our mentee while speaking down to them from the stage, but instead walk next to them through life experiences. They see how we treat our spouse and kids. They notice how we drive our car and talk to strangers. They also have a platform to discuss issues they are dealing with and sometimes just having us listen means more than us always having an answer.

The Apostle Paul told the young church in Corinth to, "follow my example, as I follow the example of Christ" (see I Corinthians 11:1). This powerful verse mentions two truths: first, Paul is carrying the weight of responsibility for someone else. He is saying that he is living a life that can be watched and imitated. He is making choices and using words that others should do and say. Paul is also saying that the source of his inspiration is Christ himself. So, Paul, who is not perfect, is following Jesus' example, who is perfect! What better truth can we offer our mentees than that? As we use Christ's life as the ultimate template for our lives, we also make ourselves a guide from the side for our mentees so they can watch our walk and imitate what a Christ-centric life looks like.

Hopefully, it gives you some relief to know that God is not calling you to be an authoritarian leader who stands over your mentee while confronting them about the many ways they are blowing it with their life choices. Instead, rest assured, that He is in control and desires to use your care and thoughtfulness for your mentee to minister well. Let our prayer be today that as we daily walk with Christ, we will invite our mentees to also walk with us.

THE SEATED SOUL

27

PROBLEM:

Our world is full of aimless and anxious youth looking for ways to define and justify their existence. Mentors with insecurities rooted in self-esteem issues or immaturity are not only ineffective; they can create toxic environments and damage a mentee's development.

PRINCIPLE:

Confident and accessible mentors striving to be a "seated soul" will build trust, present an ideal example, and create an environment of life change.

PASSAGE:

"I will lie down and sleep in peace; for you alone, O Lord, make me lie down in safety." (Psalm 4:8)

PRACTICE:

- Do a mental evaluation. Would you define yourself as a "seated soul"? What's your biggest fear/doubt/ worry right now? How is it affecting your ability to present yourself as a calm and peaceful presence while spending time with your mentee?

- Hand it over. Whether you are processing a major life event or weighed down by mundane duties, hit your knees and hand it all over to God.

I sat across the table from Neil at Lucky Dragon Chinese Restaurant in small town, Texas. He was the pastor of a large church on the highway outside Houston, and I was a veteran youth minister contemplating the idea of working with Neil in the future. Neil spoke my language as he, too, had a background in youth ministry. In fact, he was a bit of a shock-jock in the early days of his career. He would speak at large conferences, addressing auditoriums full of noisy youth who traveled in church buses to worship with a praise band and listen to Neil share funny and blunt stories from the Bible about how God wanted them to take their faith seriously. While getting other peoples' opinions on him, I learned Neil was a bit of a polarizing character in ministry during his touring days.

You either loved him or you hated him.

One of his most-famous sermon illustrations involved his lighting a cigarette on stage to make his point. (Just imagine how many youth leaders in the 80s metaphorically dropped their monocles into their tea when Neil lit up a Marlboro right after everyone was singing "Light the Fire" moments earlier.)

For as much as he was a self-proclaimed cage rattler, my lunch with Neil didn't include any shock-jock material. But, somewhere between the egg drop soup and sesame chicken, it did include his coining the phrase, "a seated soul."

It was a timely and profound metaphor for how to live a life as I was struggling to hear God's voice and follow His lead for the next big ministry direction at the time. As I sat listening to the middle-aged pastor talk about what it means to operate from a place of confident security and intention, I was reminded of Archimedes' theory of man needing "a place to stand and a lever to operate."

In short, this notion means we all need a deep-seated identity (a place to stand) and a clear purpose (a lever to operate) to be fulfilled. Isn't that one of the best gifts about ourselves that we could offer our mentees? Think about just how comforting it is to be in the same room with someone who is relaxed, confident, considerate, and easy going. Now think about the opposite of that when you are trying to have a conversation with someone who is nervous, twitchy, and unsettled.

Many of our mentees spend most of their lives with people lacking margin and who are very unseated in themselves. Some of the toughest times in my personal upbringing included times I interacted with a stepfather who was very much an unseated soul. He self-medicated with alcohol and drug abuse and it created an uneasy dynamic in my home. It is one reason why I want time with my mentee to feel calm and reassuring, even if I've had a bad day up to that point.

Would you describe yourself as a "seated soul"? Are you confident in your identity? Are you, like Solomon, praying for wisdom? What are you doing to remain as one who rests in the Lord instead of living anxious and stressed?

In Psalm 4:8, David says, "I will lie down and sleep in peace; for you alone, O Lord, make me lie down in safety." A seated soul is one that knows it can rest in the Lord because He is near!

What's your biggest fear/doubt/worry right now? Is it affecting your ability to present yourself as a calm and peaceful presence while spending time with your mentee? If after being honest with yourself, you discover that you are processing a major life situation, like the death of a loved one, or maybe even the fallout from a pandemic, it is time to get on your knees (literally) and give the issue to God. He wants your fears and doubts and anxieties. He can bear them and more importantly, he can remove them so you no longer feel responsible for them.

God does not want us jumping up and running around trying to stay busy so we can avoid dealing with our junk. He wants us to call on His name and experience a freedom that allows us to live as a seated soul and serve our mentees well.

THE PARADE PERSPECTIVE

28

PROBLEM:

Our mentees live with nearsighted vision. While they care about their future, they burn much more energy on things that in a year from now may not even exist (tests, boyfriends, sport season). Some of the biggest mistakes of our mentees' lives will be the ones they make without taking a beat and waiting for clear thought and perspective to influence their responses to a situation.

PRINCIPLE:

The work of the mentor is often simply revealing that a future beyond the present struggle exists, and it is wonderful.

PASSAGE:

"Take captive every thought to make it obedient to Christ." (2 Corinthians 10:5)

PRACTICE:

Teach your mentee the SAFE method:

- STOP yourself the next time you are feeling overwhelmed by a temporary issue. Go straight to God in prayer and ask for His perspective on the matter.

- ASK for His perspective on the matter. Allow His presence to comfort your soul and slow your heart rate. Remember that He is good and He can be trusted. May we, as people with a highly defined identity in Christ, be a wellspring of comfort to those needing to develop it in their lives.

- FIND the source of your frustration. God may reveal something you had no idea was bothering you.

- EXPRESS the need to your mentor so they can know how to pray for you.

It is difficult to tell the difference between what is eternal and what is merely temporal. Some days seem to last forever. Some people never seem to change. Things get even tougher when we throw a good measure of fear and emotion into the equation. It's these two culprits that affect us like nothing else. How often do we make rash decisions based on a high degree of fear, our own emotions, or without taking time to gather more information?

Some of the biggest mistakes of our mentees' lives will be the ones they make without taking a beat and waiting for clear thought and perspective to influence their responses to a situation.

What an incredibly practical tool Paul gave the Corinthians (and us), when he instructed to, "Take captive every thought to make it obedient to Christ." No matter your faith tradition, we probably all learned about the direct connection between our thoughts, words, and actions while growing up. You probably even gained a working definition of what sin is as being any thought, word, or action that doesn't please God.

Have you ever heard the old saying about the connection between our thoughts and our character?

Be careful of your thoughts,
For your thoughts become your words.
Be careful of your words,
For your words become your actions.
Be careful of your actions,
For your actions become your habits.
Be careful of your habits,
For your habits become your character.

Imagine living your life in such a way that even the smallest decisions would echo in some way for eternity. I don't think that's over-spiritualizing anything. As Paul was encouraging the young church, we too, should help our mentees remember that as thoughts get entertained in their minds, they can run each through a filter or lens to evaluate if it is life-giving or life-threatening. This is especially helpful for young men who seem to transform hurt and sadness so quickly into anger and aggression.

While in college, I drove by the full student parking lot of a local high school on a weekday. Police cars, ambulances, and fire engines were everywhere. An unthinkable thing had taken place just hours earlier that morning and the body of a young girl was found in her parked car. The story that was released just days later was heartbreaking. Apparently, the girl's boyfriend broke up with her and instead of seeking the help of a friend, teacher, or counselor, she walked out to her car and ended her life.

It's shocking to think that a thing like that could happen, but teenagers lacking support and perspective make decisions like this every day. All because the temporal and eternal can seem like the same thing in the heat of the moment. How significant would it have been to spend an hour listening to that young girl as she shared her pain, tears, and emptiness? Imagine how vital it could have been to speak truth, ask questions, and value her heart—giving her a glimpse at how much circumstances would improve a year from now, a week from now, or even by the next morning? That young lady was not alone in her fears and hurt, but she did not know that.

Mentors and mentees often see the same thing from a different perspective. It's like attending a big parade downtown. Your mentee sits on the curb and only gets to enjoy what she sees right in front of her from the ground level. You, however, take an elevator to a tall building which gives you the luxury of seeing all the floats and marching bands from the beginning and end of the parade. So even while your mentee is struggling to enjoy what she's seeing, you can affirm her that good things are coming right around the bend.

Now, I hope that you first connect the parade to the metaphor of how God looks at the entirety of our lives while we don't have the ability to do so. I hope the imagery gives you a peace and trust in who He is for you, His child. But I also hope you feel inspired to offer words of wisdom to your mentee as one who has lived more life and seen God work amazingly through an array of circumstances.

May we, as people with a highly defined identity in Christ, be a wellspring of comfort to those needing to develop it in their lives.

MUSCLE AND
GREY HAIR

29

PROBLEM:

Mentors believe the lie that they have nothing to offer because they are too old, not cool enough, or irrelevant.

PRINCIPLE:

God designed us for community. That means young mentees, who are strong, need the wisdom of their mentors, while mentors, who have experience and margin, benefit from the youthful energy and enthusiasm of their mentees.

PASSAGE:

"The glory of young men is their strength, but the splendor of old men is their gray hair." (Proverbs 20:29)

PRACTICE:

Make it a point to share Proverbs 20:29 at your next mentor/mentee meeting. Remind your mentee that even though you're glad you get to invest in their life, you also benefit from the friendship.

"It was the driver of the boat." That's always what any grown man tells me whenever I talk about how I'm no good at getting up and out of the water on a slalom ski or wakeboard. What they're saying is it's not because my arms aren't strong enough, it's instead because whoever was throttling the boat pulling me wasn't doing it right. It's always very nice of them to deflect the blame like that.

A few years back, my wife and I were waterskiing with friends on Lake Travis in Austin. The funniest thing happened in the middle of the day after everybody had turns behind the boat: I got tired. I had, of course, gotten tired many times before this moment, but that was the first time I had to stop doing something that I wanted to do because my body just couldn't go anymore. The exhaustion snuck up on me and rudely let me know that I was getting older. I was twenty-seven.

Proverbs 20:29 says that a young man's glory is in his strength and an old man's beauty is in his gray hair. This verse almost reveals itself like a math equation. There is a symmetry and equal value between two different types of people, the young and the old. Both young and old enjoy substantial identity but their purpose is found in two different places. We can also gather a logical interpretation from the verse, as it can refer to two separate people living at the same time in history, or to one person transitioning from youth to old age. When you are young, you are strong. You possess strength because your body is fresh and able. But you don't have wisdom because you have yet to acquire the knowledge and experience that combine to form it. As you age and your wisdom increases, so your body's strength and ability decrease. But *community* gets a shout out in this verse as well because it reminds us that the young, though they are strong, desperately need older people in their lives showing them what it means to live rightly beyond their youthful ignorance. Our older generations benefit from young peoples' strength, and they can find the sweet spot in their lives once they are investing in young people as mentors.

Without this perspective, we risk young people becoming so eager to be adults that they bypass the innocence and fun that should be part of growing up, focusing instead on the seriousness of staring at their phones all day as they fret over social media and yearn for dating relationships that progress too quickly in hopes of experiencing adult things before they are ready. Similarly, many grown adults aren't ready to give up the benefits of youth, so they color their gray hair and dress as if they are thirty years younger. It's like spending the first half of one's life wanting to be older, only to spend the second half wanting to be younger. The real problem is that you never get to enjoy the contentment that comes from living in the present moment.

Purposeful living develops naturally over time. Our strength may wane, but our wisdom should flourish. It makes sense that when we are young, we are completely concerned with ourselves. Even with parents, mentors, and ministers investing in us, we remain in a state of soaking up attention and energy, rarely considering the idea that we can be rivers instead of lakes. This is what Richard Rohr calls "the first half of our lives", when we are constructing the container we will use in the second half to live purposefully and serve others.

The issue for many is they never stop living from this first half of life source, so they never go on to live in the fullness that a seasoned purpose reveals to us. It's as if they omit the part when Jesus said that those coming after him must first take up their cross before they are freed up to follow Him.

Make it a point to share Proverbs 20:29 at your next mentor/mentee meeting. Remind your mentee that even though you're glad you get to invest in their life, you also benefit from the friendship.

The Bible is full of examples of intergenerational ministry. Whether it's Moses and Joshua, Naomi and Ruth, or Paul and Timothy, God's model for growth is a mutual exchange between the generations. We often draw distinctions between baby boomers, gen x, millennials and gen-z, but the truth is—we are all called to work together in harmony, sharing wisdom from one era to the next. Ultimately, it is the plan laid out in scripture, and it should be the plan we adopt as well, as Malachi wrote, "He will turn the hearts of the parents to their children, and the hearts of the children to their parents..." (Malachi 4:6).

MENTORING IS BASEBALL

30

PROBLEM:

Mentors get discouraged and believe they are ineffective if every encounter with their mentee isn't a great time with obvious progress being made.

PRINCIPLE:

Know that you will have awkward moments with your mentee, but staying encouraged and getting up when you fall down is how you mentor for the long haul.

PASSAGE:

"The godly may trip seven times, but they will get up again. But one disaster is enough to overthrow the wicked." (Proverbs 24:16)

PRACTICE:

- Recalibrate your expectations and remember that not every hang out has to be a homerun. Striking out is part of the process and we should intentionally factor that into our approach and mindset.

- Be deliberate about judging your mentoring sessions in a fair light. It's ok to just have an ok hang-out!

- Focus on showing up and doing your part. Trust that the Lord will provide the breakthrough in his perfect timing.

Baseball, or as some people call it, "America's pastime," is such an interesting game. There is something about the game of baseball that just screams summertime, late sunsets, popsicles, sunflower seeds. Maybe that's why baseball was my first love.

I can remember when I first started playing baseball, I tried to hit a home run every single time. I'd get up to the plate, lock eyes with the pitcher, and swing as hard as an eight-year-old could swing. Sure, I made contact every so often, but, more times than not, I struck out.

Needless to say, I quickly got pretty disappointed. *Maybe baseball isn't the game for me afterall,* I'd think to myself.

And disappointment is the first step in abandoning your post in any walk of life. Here's how it goes:

You have a failure or setback.

You get disappointed.

You don't want to try as hard or get back up after the failure.

The lies show up saying, "You're no good," or "You can't do this."

You start thinking about quitting.

That's what happened with me in the game of baseball. It wasn't until a coach pulled me aside and truly explained the game of baseball to me that I began to see myself and my actions clearly. In learning the game, I realized that just hitting the ball is a great place to start.

Did you know that the batting average of every baseball player in the hall of fame is a combined and averaged out amounts to .303. That means if you hit the ball 303 out of 1,000 times at bat, you are considered one of the greatest baseball players of all time. That's 697 misses!

3 out of every 10 makes a great baseball player.

And I could say the same is true for mentoring.

When I first became a mentor, I wanted a home run every time. I thought my mentee would love me, tell me how great I was, and earn straight A's while getting a full ride to Harvard. When those things didn't happen, I got disappointed.

After a while, I adjusted my definition of success.

Just hanging out with my mentee was a base hit. A single, if you will.

A smile was a double.

A laugh was a triple.

A solid conversation was a home run.

I focused on plate appearances, not homeruns.

I trusted that the Lord would do what he does if I just kept getting up to the plate.

3 out of every 10.

If you can have a great hang out or deep conversation 3 out of every 10 times, I'd say that'll put you in the mentoring hall of fame.

The more swings the better, as the more you swing, the more chances you get at contact. Just like the more you hang out with your mentee, the more chances you get at connecting.

You're going to strike out. Focus on getting back up and taking another swing instead of fixating on the negative. Don't worry about swinging for the fences or home runs. Just focus on taking your swings and seeing what happens. Dial in on what you *can* control.

Your mentee will not experience some dramatic breakthrough everytime you are together. There is usually a *buildup* before a breakthrough. Buildup can feel mundane, simple, unimportant, or like a strike out altogether. Nevertheless, it is contributing toward eventual breakthrough and progress with your mentee.

So instead of seeing your "strike out" as a failure, see it as a necessary step toward getting on base and making a lasting difference. Mentoring is baseball.

ZACH GARZA is passionate about relationships because the Lord used relationships to change his life. He has been a part of multiple mentoring non-profit organizations and now focuses his time on helping others in the realm of mentoring, discipleship, and fathering.

His days are spent investing in servant-leaders who invest in others. His joy is to add value through guiding others to overcome their obstacles and encouraging them to see themselves how God sees them.

Zach and his wife Sara live in Waco, Texas with their three children Zach Jr., Stephen, and Joanna. He loves spending time with his family, playing basketball, and eating tacos. Zach is also a consultant and keynote speaker for ministries and non-profits and would be honored to help you in any way that he can.

Learn more at:

www.YouCanMentor.com and www.RaisingUpFathers.com

or you can contact him at:

Zach@YouCanMentor.com or @youcanmentor

You Can Mentor.

RAISING UP
TEN THOUSAND
FATHERS

JOHN BARNARD was born and raised in South Houston, Texas. Shortly after receiving his undergrad from Texas Tech, he began a twenty-year career in ministry which included roles as associate pastor, worship pastor, and youth minister in Lubbock, Austin, Houston, and rural Texas. He completed a master's in church leadership in 2012.

In 2005, John started mentoring skateboarders by building relationships, sharing his faith, and producing and giving away skateboards. Seven years later, he established Middleman Skateboard Ministries as a board-run nonprofit.

John and his wife, Mandi, moved their family to Waco to run Middleman as a full-time mentoring ministry in 2016. Today, Middleman focuses its efforts on local mentoring and supporting other skate ministries across the country by offering free resources, strategy, counseling, and financial support.

To find out more about Middleman or to contact John:

middleman-ministries.org

@middlemanskateboards

MIDDLEMAN  **MINISTRIES**

You Can Mentor.

- **Listen to the "You Can Mentor" podcast**
- **Come to the National Christian Mentoring Gathering**
- **Check out our resources and build relationships with other mentoring leaders**

We help Christian mentors & mentoring organizations thrive

www.youcanmentor.com

hello@youcanmentor.com

@youcanmentor

www.ingramcontent.com/pod-product-compliance
Lightning Source LLC
LaVergne TN
LVHW041317080426
835513LV00008B/498